Find your passion,
Pursue your vision
and make your mark
on the world. Enjoy
the ride.

Steve Coats

10/09/08

THERE IS NO
BOX

Discovering the Internal Character Needed to Achieve Groundbreaking Growth.

by **Steve Coats** and **Tom Heuer**

For permission requests, contact the publisher at:

Executive Excellence Publishing   Distributed by Bookworld
1806 North 1120 West
Provo, UT 84604
Phone: 1-801-375-4060
Toll Free: 1-877-250-1983
Fax: 1-801-377-5960
www.eep.com www.leaderexcel.com

For Executive Excellence books, magazines and other products,
contact Executive Excellence directly. Call 1-877-250-1983,
fax 1-801-377-5960, or visit our websites at www.eep.com or
www.LeaderExcel.com.

First edition.
Printed in the United States of America
10 9 8 7 6 5 4 3 2 1

$19.95 USA
Business/Leadership
ISBN 1-930771-28-2

Advance Praise for *There Is No Box*

Experience is the best teacher—if you're willing to learn from it. And that's just what Steve Coats and Tom Heuer enable you to do. *There Is No Box* is all about the passion, competence, courage, and commitment that it takes to challenge, innovate, and grow. It's a fun read, full of real-life tales of experimentation and risk and practical tips to prepare you for growth. Buy, it, use it, and learn from it.

—Jim Kouzes, Coauthor of the bestselling *The Leadership*
  Challenge **and** *A Leader's Legacy*

Coats and Heuer offer fresh perspective on change as well as a new understanding of what characteristics drive ground-breaking innovation. This book is essential reading for anyone serious about growth and success.

—Nancy L. Zimpher, President, University of Cincinnati

This is a must read for everyone that wants to understand the opportunities that every organization has but few realize. Real life examples and lessons, if followed, will enable extraordinary results.

—Emerson Brumback, President and COO, M&T Bank

Steve and Tom make us hold up the mirror and ask ourselves, do we really want to grow, change and develop as leaders? Do we have the passion and courage to not look around at others…but to say, "Do I want it bad enough?" Am I part of the solution or the problem? It's a great read for anyone who wants to make a difference!

—Lauris Woolford, Sr. Vice President, Executive Coaching,
  Fifth Third Bank

Dedication

There Is No Box is dedicated to all those restless people who are willing to take the risks necessary to move beyond the way things have always been done and make a better place for customers, work organizations, communities, perhaps even the world at large. They do not simply think outside the proverbial box, they don't recognize the existence of this box of limitations to begin with. And thus, they find a way to break through the constraints that seem to hold many other people back.

About the Title: *There Is No Box*

Whenever people anywhere are challenged to come up with something substantially new, from a breakthrough product idea to an innovative solution for a knotty problem, they are frequently offered the same guidance. You have no doubt heard it and are perhaps even numbed by it now. People are told, *think outside the box*.

Surprisingly, we found that people who are very effective at producing lasting growth opportunities seldom subscribe to that advice. We first began to understand this when we interviewed Jim Bonaminio, founder of the highly successful international market (and idea factory) Jungle Jim's in Fairfield, OH. In a preliminary meeting with Sarah Kaufmann, one of Jim's close associates, she shared with us that Jim's creativity and constant growth ideas did not come from "thinking outside the box," because he did not believe in a box to begin with.

Since then we have met and heard about many people who, like Jim, do not attempt to *box in their thinking* in any fashion. For people like them, there is no box. Think about that notion for a moment.

We certainly thought about it, and here is what we discovered. The *proverbial box* is a human creation. Innovation and growth become stymied because people have created "boxes" full of seemingly unchangeable methods, incorrect assumptions, invalid beliefs and other limitations that prevent or prohibit breakthrough thinking.

True growth leaders refuse to burden themselves with a self-imposed *box of limitations*. They do not accept that there needs to be such a box. Rather, they continue to focus their attention on the *outcomes* they are pursuing. They look forward into the future rather than backwards into a box. And they find new sources of energy and inspiration to overcome the inevitable adversity they encounter along the way. Refusing to accept the box does not mean being naive and denying the existence of legitimate barriers. It means choosing a course that centers on more forward-looking, possibility thinking.

We heard an interesting comment from an interview with Howard Schultz, the CEO of Starbucks. He described his life as a young boy, when he lived "in the Projects" in Brooklyn. His family had little money, and his father had been laid off due to a work-related injury. It was a pretty hopeless situation. When asked what he wished for at that time, he replied that his dream was simply to get out. He could not conceive of anything bigger or more future-oriented than that at the time.

Sometimes when people feel imprisoned in some way, the only thing they can think about is breaking free.

As we reflected on Schultz's comments about his difficult younger years, we began to wonder about the ill effects on people when, day after day, they are told they need to "think outside the box." Obviously, they are seen by others as being clearly stuck within the box, or they would not continue to be directed to get out of the box. Might they begin to believe they are stuck in a box as well?

If that is the case, might it then be possible for people who feel stuck within the box to become like Schultz and focus solely on simply breaking out of it, instead of concentrating on real growth opportunities? Might they begin to wonder if there even *is* a way out? Is it possible that they might gradually begin to find comfort inside those self-imposed walls, and thus, quit heeding the calls to move out? Perhaps they have ventured out before and been beaten back. Maybe they have never tried because they don't believe they have the capabilities of imagination and fresh thinking, to move successfully out into the intimidating, even frightening, frontiers of new challenges and growth opportunities. Just keep in mind, whatever the reason, the result will be little or no innovation and growth.

You may think we are stretching the whole *box* notion a little too far, or that the idea of *no box* is pretty much the same as thinking outside the box. We hope you will reflect on the differences. However, the purpose of this book is not to debate the issue. It is to introduce you to the character attributes that enable people to move far beyond all kinds of limitations in order to produce new possibilities for themselves and their organizations. We invite you to become more like the examples we found, and learn what you must have in order to let go of the box and experience groundbreaking growth.

About the Symbolism Behind the Moving Ripples of Water

A unique property of water is to take the shape of that which surrounds it but to never possess a specific shape by itself. As Mircea Eliade notes in *The Sacred & The Profane*, this is so because water is incapable of transcending its own mode of being and of manifesting itself in forms.

These qualities of humidity and fluidity give water a symbolism of *potentialities which are unmanifested and undifferentiated* rather than realized and actualized. Whereas earth symbolizes the embodiment of form, water symbolizes the dissolution of form into a mass of *possibilities*. Eliade comments about this symbolism of potentials, noting: "The waters symbolize the universal sum of virtualities; they are . . . 'spring and origin,' the reservoir of all possibilities of existence; they precede every form and support every creation."

The potential for groundbreaking growth within us is like the ripples of water uniformly moving out from a single drop. There are unlimited possibilities for those ripples to reach different, unmanifested destinations. Once tapped and allowed to reach the surface, the internal character for growth (as described in this book) can also have unlimited possibilities, assume many forms, and help you achieve your goals.

CONTENTS

PART ONE: THE FOUNDATION OF GROWTH

"The 'surplus society' has a surplus of similar companies, employing sim-ilar people, with similar educational backgrounds, coming up with similar ideas, producing similar things, with similar prices and similar quality."
—Kjell Nordstrom and Jonas Ridderstrale, *Funky*

INTRODUCTION

In June 2005, General Motors announced the layoff of 25,000 workers as part of a necessary $2.5 billion multi-year cost reduction. One of the factors they cited was that the cost of employee health care added nearly $1,500 to the cost of each car produced, making it much tougher to compete. Interestingly enough, one analyst following GM commented that if the company were selling a million more cars each year, the health care cost would not be much of a factor.

GM was not alone. At the same time Delta Airlines, and many of the other large carriers, were petitioning Congress for relief from their pension contribution obligations. They just did not have the money to both pay for pensions they had promised and continue to run the business. By this time most of the big airline companies had either filed or threatened to file for bankruptcy.

If there is a single issue that has the attention of nearly every leader and organization right now, it is *growth*. Mergers and acquisitions will always be one way to grow, as will geographic expansion. But will either of these be the only savior for GM, the airlines or most other well-established companies? Probably not. They have to figure out new ways to grow. They have to find some way to add new value to current or new groups of customers, in order to sustain and increase the profitability of their businesses.

And that value will not come solely from cost containment or process improvement initiatives. The age of Six Sigma is past as most great companies have already completed this work. Today is the age of innovation and creativity. The focus must be on moving the enterprise to the next level of growth.

For growth to occur, people must change what they do and how they do it, sometimes very dramatically. And that is the core of the issue. It is uncomfortable and just plain hard for people, let alone organizations, to challenge the normal way of doing things and change. We have worked with companies that have laid out extraordinarily ambitious growth plans with sales growth targeted in the 20 percent to 40 percent range, year after year. And we see people (and organizations for that matter) continue to do exactly the same things in exactly the same way and wonder why they continually fall short. It takes more than a 20 to 40 percent increase in sales calls per week, or adding 20 to 40 percent more non-valued added features to current products, or launching a bunch of new offerings that no one wants, to achieve ambitious objectives. It takes real change.

Several years ago, economist Paul Romer introduced an economic concept called the *New Growth Theory*. The essential point of the *New Growth Theory* is that knowledge drives growth. Because ideas can be infinitely shared and reused, we can accumulate them without limit. They are not subject to what economists call diminishing returns. Instead, the increasing returns on knowledge can continuously propel economic growth—for nations, firms and individuals.

Romer might also say that *growth* is just another word for *change*.

Hence, for companies to grow, they must change. And to do that, they must have people who are capable of both conceiving and leading those changes. Growth through acquisition is often an important but expensive component of a viable overall strategy, but think twice if you believe it is the only option. For organizations to grow, they must continue to find, develop and capitalize on unique advantages in the marketplace. Sustainable advantage is never an entitlement, nor is it achieved by standing still in a changing world. It takes people who accept the challenge of changing the rules of the game, people with great curiosity, fresh ideas, imagination, innovative thinking and of course, the courage to ultimately follow through and make change happen.

There is an almost never-ending lament by many people about the amount of change occurring in the world. Listen closely and you will hear them long for things to "settle down" and get back to normal. We hope they realize that the *new normal* is in fact *constant change*.

As some hopelessly await a return to a more comfortable past, others are contributing to the turmoil. They are actively looking for and pursuing ways to change things—to grow their organizations in new ways, or to make either their world or "the world" a better place. They are constantly striving to take other people to new heights by accomplishing something never done before. These people are often referred to as leaders.

For most of our careers, we have worked with a variety of companies, either as actual employees or outside consultants, focusing on leadership development. We have always believed that great leadership was required for growth, especially in tough times. Since September 11th 2001, along with the bubble burst in the stock market, rising oil prices and a general wariness about the future, sustaining a business over the long haul has become a daunting challenge. When things are swirling around you at a dizzying pace, and you feel like you are standing on quicksand, trying to "manage" your organizations to greatness simply won't work any longer. It takes something more.

Management scholar Peter Drucker noted that only three things occur naturally in organizations—friction, confusion and underperformance. Everything else requires leadership. Although we chuckled a bit when we first read this, we have learned that Mr. Drucker was right on target, as usual. Since growth was not in his list of natural occurrences, we concluded it requires leadership. Does it ever!

Regardless of the source, a common action associated with leaders is their propensity to challenge the way other people think or what they do. A case in point is the breakthrough work of researchers and authors Jim Kouzes and Barry Posner (*The Leadership Challenge*), who conceived *The Five Practices of Exemplary Leadership®*. One of the practices they found consistent in leaders who accomplish extraordinary things was what they called *Challenge the Process®*. They went on to more clearly and behaviorally define *Challenge* as "search for opportunities by seeking innovative ways to grow, and improve, and to experiment and take risks by constantly generate small wins and learn from mistakes."

The people we most admire as leaders challenge the way things are done. Like Kouzes and Posner, we have never met anyone who said they did their best as a leader when merely managing the status quo. Whatever the reasons, from simple curiosity to dissatisfaction with the current state, they worked at creating change. And more often than not, those changes led to new growth opportunities.

Sometimes the challenges that leaders attempt to take on are rather sizable, like revising the way children across the country become educated, or completely refocusing a major corporation on a new way of doing business. Other times the scope is smaller, like persuading members of a church to accept new ways of serving those in need, or getting a boss to streamline or eliminate redundant reports. No matter the scale of what is being tackled—be it steps in a process, products to offer or markets to serve, or even the well-entrenched mindsets of other people—leaders always need to challenge conventional thinking in order to accomplish the extraordinary. That is especially true in seeking extraordinary growth.

It is a good thing leaders do challenge. For growth is the lifeblood of any business that hopes to survive over time. Challenging and consequently improving the way things are done is the practice that drives profitable growth. Yet ironically, we have found that although many people believe in the importance of challenge, cultural norms make it extremely difficult for these people to be successful in their attempts to improve and grow their areas of responsibility. Perhaps you have experienced some of the resistance, described in comments such as:

- We have done this way for years and have always made money.

- If you keep trying to buck the system, you are going to get labeled as not being a team player.
- If you would stop trying to change everything and simply do your job, you would be a lot better off.
- The people at the top have the answers, so just listen to them.

Have you heard some of these before?

All of this has led us to a couple of conclusions. First, we believe that great companies understand the lasting value of organic growth and have learned how to grow. Dell, for example, has become a $40 billion company in 20 years, and has organically grown market share 180 percent from 2000 to 2005. By the way, these astounding results have been achieved in spite of Michael Dell being told several years ago that his business model was not scalable.

We have also concluded that most organizations have more than enough managers, whose main goals seem to be stability, comfort, and a heavily skewed focus on today's results. In fact, the requirement for short term results and the "ease" of growing through M&A has caused many organizations to shun organic growth. They simply do not know how to do it and don't seem to be attempting to do much to build that capability.

Totally, all organizations need more growth leaders—at every level. They need more people who will view the world differently, conceive new possibilities, offer innovative options, and lead others to achieve higher levels of performance. Organizations need more people who will challenge the way things get done, and navigate through the maze of real and cultural barriers they face. Without these people, ongoing profitable growth, perhaps even survival, would be at risk.

There is one final and very important conclusion we have reached, which is the major theme of this book: *The willingness to go out on a limb and take on the seemingly immovable forces of the status quo requires a person to have and rely on a few, very specific, internal character attributes. Without them, the road to prosperity and growth is more difficult, if not impossible. Even if the organization provides great technology, systems, financial support and such, growth will flounder if these character attributes are not pervasive.*

As tough as this may be to accept, we have observed that organizations continue to spend more effort on the external side of growth than the internal. The major focus is usually on equipping people with the knowledge of what they should do and how they should it, and with the organizational resources and systems needed to execute. There is much less effort directed toward helping people understand and more fully develop the essential character attributes, the all-important seeds which set the entire growth process into motion.

That is why we wrote this book. We have identified the internal character attributes most needed for producing groundbreaking growth opportunities—for you and the various organizations you may be part of. And we gladly share them with you because we love facilitating the growth of individuals and organizations. We believe that people become renewed and energized when they choose to achieve something new, different or unique. We know that business organizations are more vibrant places to work when they are actively growing, and we truly enjoy getting to know about people who have shaken up, if not flat out obliterated "the way it has always been done." We also feel great disappointment, even sadness at the number of companies whose growth engines are sputtering. We desire to help you get your engine re-tuned and racing forward again.

By applying the principles of growth, you will become better prepared to meet the challenges awaiting you. Along the way, you will better understand why sometimes you, or those around you, are reluctant to tackle new things or volunteer the ideas and effort to break the logjams that block growth. You will have a valuable way to assess the risk-taking and innovation vitality of your company's culture, crucial for sustaining desired results.

Keep this in mind as well. The need for challenging conventional standards to find new solutions is not just limited to organizations. It is vital for individuals in their personal lives as well. In the following pages, you will read about growth leaders who have made enormous differences and created new opportunities in communities, schools, and business organizations.

Just think about all the things that you take for granted today, that not long ago were considered impossibilities. The concept of the telephone was scorned. It was obvious that man could not fly — let alone to the moon. A worker's job was to comply not to think, or be directly involved in decisions. And of course the concept of a world wide web for instantly retrieving information from anywhere around the world could be nothing more than pure science fiction. Now think about the massive impact these and other innovations have had on the world. Thank goodness that some people believed the future could be different and better, accepted the challenge to do something about it, and struggled to make it a reality.

Buckminster Fuller once wrote, "On spaceship earth there are no passengers, only crew." When it comes to growth in any aspect of your life or business, do not remain a passenger who is just along for the ride. Choose to be a growth leader who will step out beyond today's established boundaries and accept the challenge of creating a new tomorrow. You will find it an exciting and rewarding adventure.

Chapter 1: A Different Approach

Profitable growth will not occur from continuing to do the same old things in the same old ways. Things must change. The greatest changes that are produced by people usually come from challenging an accepted, conventional norm, whether the norm is paddling by hand into a wave, designing cars like a box, or offering new medications in the same fashion as old ones.

Example 1. Picture yourself walking down a street surrounded by buildings seven stories tall. Suddenly, these buildings start crashing down all around you. No matter how fast you move, they keep collapsing right at your heels. And, you know if you trip or fall, you will be immediately crushed.

Sound like something out of a nightmare? Not if you are Laird Hamilton, as this fairly accurately describes a major part of his life. In actuality, Laird is not being chased by falling steel and concrete, but by 70-foot high crashing walls of water. For you see, Laird is a big wave surfer, and the first of only a few people who have ever ridden a wave of that size.

You might have trouble imagining just how high a 70-foot wave is. So, stop in at a high-rise hotel with an open-air lobby, ride the elevator to the 7th floor, get off and look down over the railing toward the ground. That is the breathtaking drop that a surfer faces when at the top of a big wave.

Until just a few years ago, no one had ever conquered a wave of this size. In fact, this challenge of surfing was referred to as the "unridden realm," and Laird was determined to ride it. No one knew if it was possible to actually surf this size of wave, because it was physically impossible to even get properly positioned on it to try.

If you have ever watched people surfing, you are aware how they get started on their ride. The lay flat on their boards and paddle like crazy, until they reach a point on the front of the wave where momentum and gravity take over and they can stand up and ride.

Here was the problem for Laird and other big-wave surfers. Because of their size, these monster waves moved too fast for anyone to be able to paddle onto them. Like being unable to drive a car, because of no key to start the engine, Laird knew that to ride such a wave, he needed to figure out how to first get onto it. And that is precisely what he did.

How do you think he did it? Did he substantially increase his already astonishing conditioning regimen in order to paddle faster? Did he charter a boat to take him out a mile from shore, so he could slowly drift in and hope he found himself on the right wave? Did he just parachute in from the skies above.

None of these options were the solution, although believe it or not, the parachute concept was not that far off. Rather than dropping onto a big wave from an airplane, Laird towed into it, being pulled behind a Jet Ski like a water skier on a surfboard. Now being able to reach a speed of nearly 40 mph, Laird found the key to the unridden realm, and proved that a seven-story wave could indeed be successfully ridden. Big-wave surfing was forever changed, and a big-wave controversy was immediate born. More about that later.

Example 2. Halfway around the world in Munich, Germany, another man was changing another timeless institution. And although his mission was not surfing a 70-foot high wall of water, it was every bit as daunting. In fact, the innovations he was spurring were so dramatic that on-line petitions soon appeared. Thousands of people were signing up to express their disapproval and request he be fired.

Imagine going to work for a company that has one of the best success rates and well-deserved reputations of any company in the world. The quality of BMW automobiles sets them apart, putting them in a category with only the best-engineered cars in the world. For that reason, they have been enormously popular. And BMW's have always been easy to identify, with their signature black, blue and white nameplate and their "box-like" design.

If you are not a BMW enthusiast, you may have never heard of Chris Bangle. Bangle, an American from the Midwest, who at one time considered a vocation in the ministry, became the Chief Designer of the BMW Group a few years back. His design responsibility included some of BMW's most well known automobiles, 7-Series, 6-Series, 5-Series, Z4, X3 and 1-Series. From the moment he accepted the position, he was under fire.

For years the BMW had been regarded as one of the best-engineered cars in the world. The company tag line continually reminded everyone of this, describing their automobiles as the "Ultimate Driving Machine." On the other hand, their cars were never held up as the "ultimate designed machine," as people had become quite comfortable with the rather conservative, "boxy" shape.

It was Chris Bangle's responsibility to take the look of these classic cars forward. And when some of his radical new designs first appeared, BMW traditionalists, including some people in the press, literally recoiled in shock. They were not only critical of Bangle, but troubled by the BMW board's decision in hiring him in the first place.

Although many competing auto companies were attempting at the time to grow their markets with designs based on a "retro" look, Chris Bangle was designing BMW's for the future. He was applying sharper edges, and using folds, curves and creases in different ways than ever before to give the cars a dramatic new appearance. His innovative styling set the design world buzzing, earning him Man of the Year by *Automobile Magazine* in 2003. But the BMW loyalists had a much different opinion.

Like Laird Hamilton, Chris Bangle was out on the cutting edge of change. And whenever people like them set out to change something, especially something that for years have been accepted as "the only way," they face controversy and a very steep, uphill battle for acceptance.

Example 3. Hawaii and Germany are not the only places where people have been taking on the status quo and attempting to change and grow their businesses. This third example takes us right to the heart of the United States. Many people will have directly benefited from the results of this challenging endeavor, or know someone who has.

In the mid 1990's, AstraZeneca had a very successful product, the prescription medicine known as Prilosec. In a few short years, the little pill had earned a solid reputation and strong market share in the prescription medicine world for helping people with acid reflux disease.

Around 1997, as the patent protection was waning, AstraZeneca entered into an agreement with Procter & Gamble with the aspiration of jointly taking Prilosec from the prescription-only world into the OTC (over-the-counter) market. Think about the scope of this challenge. These two companies were vastly different in terms of cultures and core competencies. AstraZeneca was a pharmaceutical company, staffed with doctors and other specialists who through traditional scientific research methods, developed prescription medicines sold primarily to doctors. P&G, on the other hand, was primarily a consumer products company, known not only for its brand and marketing expertise, but also for its relentless pursuit of directly touching consumers and satisfying their needs in product categories ranging from laundry detergents to disposable diapers. Procter & Gamble also had a small but growing Health Care business staffed with scientific and medical experts, but the usual R&D timetable for Procter & Gamble was calibrated in months not years, as speed and agility were recognized competitive levers for them.

How would you like to have the task of bringing these two companies together to launch a new product? Assuming you could get these two radically different companies on the same page, you would also have to deal with the FDA (Food and Drug Administration) and the "Rubik's cube process" of getting a new drug approved by them—a drug that had never been considered for the OTC market to this point. Can you imagine all the political high wires you would have to walk, and the hundreds of things that could easily go wrong, any of which would lead to failure?

This was the 70-foot wave facing Lisa Allgood, who was the project leader of the effort to introduce Prilosec OTC. To her credit, Lisa's team was successful in getting the product launched in 2003, and it has become a blockbuster for P&G. It was the most successful first launch in the company's history and has continued to be part of P&G's success. It was clearly a growth opportunity that Lisa and her team made happen.

One thing was clear from the beginning—this was not a "business as usual" proposition. The team had to figure out what it was going to take to be successful. Although they did a lot of things in very different ways, two key deviations from the "normal approach" really fueled their success.

First, they created an entirely different structure for the team. They chose not to become a typical group, where a handful of AstraZeneca people had to frequently report into and get permission from their management, and another handful of P&G people had to do the same with their management. Instead, they created their own "phantom company," with no functional ties back to their respective lines of business. They called the joint team "The pHantom Company" (Procter Helping Astra negotiate the OTC market). They had their own goals and methods. They even went so far as to issue team "pHantom stock certificates" to symbolize their independence and unity, although they were still within the boundaries of their respective companies. They wanted everyone from both companies to feel equally invested in the success of the new product.

As you might surmise, the creation of a phantom company was not the typical approach to new products in either company!

The second change was even more significant, and might have been the biggest turning point of all. This group changed the way a prescription drug was normally brought into the OTC world. Conventional wisdom stated that an OTC drug was offered at half the dosage of the prescription drug, and was based on episodic, symptomatic occurrences, meaning the drug is taken only when it is needed. For example, when you have an "episode" of pain in the head, you take an aspirin.

Prilosec OTC was offered at the identical strength of its prescription counterpart, but differed in the duration of therapy—the amount of time it was to be taken. Prescription Prilosec was prescribed for a specific medically diagnosed condition, to be taken continuously for at least a 28-day period. Prilosec OTC was to be offered for half the duration cycle, or for a 14-day period, for the OTC treatment of frequent heartburn.

Now this might not seem like a big deal, but, it was earthshaking from an historical perspective in negotiating with the FDA. It might be comparable to getting the government to drop the income tax and move strictly to a sales tax!

If you will recall, both Laird Hamilton and Chris Bangle stirred up quite the controversy with the changes they were making. It was no different for Lisa. We will not go into all the controversies that were generated by deviating from the normal "half dosage and per episode" OTC formula, but consider this. Think about the labeling on the Prilosec OTC package. Do you think there might have been some real discussions about the required level of detailed information that needed to be provided on the package, to ensure that consumers clearly understood how to take the medication safely, and when they should consult a doctor? Is it possible that some may have thought that a full strength, two-week duration drug was just too much of a change for the average consumer to digest in the OTC world? There were, no doubt, numerous controversies of all shapes and sizes hitting the fan in a change of this magnitude.

These examples remind us of an important lesson about change and growth. In order to grow their results, workers in companies everyday are encouraged to challenge the way things are done, to take risks, even to think outside of the proverbial box. For you who have heard this litany, you know that it's not easy. There are many critics and roadblocks. Challenging the way things are done to achieve new levels of performance, and generate exciting opportunities for growth, is hard and perilous work.

Too often, the discussion about how to challenge current norms has focused on all the things a person needs to *do*. Understand what you are challenging. Find out who your opposition will be. Build an air-tight business case. Make sure you have other people to support you. Take bite-sized risks. There are many other helpful hints, and collectively they add up to some very valuable advice.

Unfortunately, focusing solely on what to do is incomplete. It's similar to hearing someone tell you that what you have to do to win a race is simply run faster than everyone else. Many times people know what to do—and even how to do it. So if it is not what they do that separates the successful challengers from the rest of the pack, what is it?

Over the years we have closely studied examples of people who have broken through the shackles of conformity and created new and better ways of accomplishing things. Rather than continuing to look deeper into what people needed to *do*, we started looking at these champions of challenge and growth from a slightly different perspective. We started observing what people first needed to *have* in order to accomplish remarkable outcomes.

Throughout this book, we will describe some of the most common attributes that these champions of growth possessed. And in case you are wondering, we did not find that they needed to have extremely deep pockets, privileged bloodlines, or vast positional power. Although external factors like these would certainly not hurt, they were seldom, if ever, a required part of the success formula.

We did find however that people who are exceptional at creating a significant change in the way things are done share some powerful, internal attributes. These attributes are familiar to all of us. You will recognize them. On the other hand, you may not live them right now. If you are willing to take an honest look at who you are, you will likely learn quite a bit about yourself. You will determine if you *have* what it takes to ultimately *do* what it takes to bring about something new.

Our guess is that in some part of your life, you have your own version of a 70-foot wave that you would like to conquer. Whether at work or in your personal life, a truly meaningful goal or desire is calling you. And right now, it is still unmet. We hope that you will soon be better equipped to go do something about it—and that you will struggle to make it a success for you and those around you.

Chapter 2: The Path We Will Follow

Have you ever stopped to think about the lessons of change that come from the human body? From the moment we are conceived, growth occurs at a lightning pace. Think about how the physical appearance of the body dramatically changes, especially during the younger, formative years. The same is true internally, as the brain and other organs grow, change and mature to serve their purposes. Even in the smaller things, whether it is the pupils of the eyes immediately dilating or constricting in response to differences in light, or the sudden appearance of goose-bumps when we get cold, the human body is nearly always in a state of development.

But look inside for a moment at body systems like temperature, blood pressure or rate of breathing. These systems are designed to stay relatively constant, and if they do vary too much or too fast, it can be fatal. When temperature goes up, muscles ache, chills set in, coughing occurs, blood pressure surges or drops, a person is considered to be sick. These are abnormal conditions. But with time, a variety of outside actions (like medicines) and the workings of the immune system, one gets well. Temperature retreats to 98.6, and breathing, blood pressure and everything else returns to normal.

For the human body to grow, it must change. It is ironic that on one hand, our bodies are designed to change, while on the other hand our bodies fight to keep certain systems exactly the same.

Our experience tells us that organizations are similar. For growth to occur, certain things must change by design, and other things must be preserved, or remain normal, forever. Unfortunately, within an organization (and outside for that matter), there is often a great deal of confusion about what can and should change and what must remain the same. This confusion can directly lead to great differences of opinions, frustrations, arguments, and even feelings of hopelessness. It is also one of the variables that slows growth and makes challenging the status quo so difficult, perhaps even terrifying.

When Laird Hamilton first began to tow-in to big waves, not everyone praised his breakthrough. Many labeled his action as cheating. They also accused him of "taking the soul out of the sport." No longer was surfing simply the skill of man against the forces of nature, but now it involved noisy, smelly machines that "made it easier." Laird and the others who found towing-in a great innovation said it was not cheating, but just different. Whether cheating or different, significant change brings forth a lot of emotion that often sparks controversy and disagreement. Be forewarned, the journey of breakthrough is never hazard-free.

The leaders who choose to take on some of these controversial battles need to have "the right stuff" if they expect to be successful. We find that much of this right stuff falls into three character groupings: commitment, competence and self-assurance. If people lack any of these, they will likely never achieve the goals they seek.

Commitment

People who successfully challenge conventional ways of doing things and lead growth are deeply committed to the challenges and changes they are pursuing. They strongly believe in their aspirations and are able to stay focused, in spite of distractions that are thrown in their way. Laird Hamilton was unswerving in his desire to ride the unridden realm. Chris Bangle was totally devoted to creating a new look for BMW. Nancy Brogan, who will be featured later in the book, was not about to let anything, including lack of funds or language barriers, stand in her way of altering the way education was provided for the poor students at her middle school. Tough challenges always require true commitment.

In the discussion of commitment, we will bring out the importance of the first two essential attributes—passion and vision. These words are casually bantered around so much these days, that people may have become numbed to their meaning. But those who take on the challenge to grow, change and improve are fully aware of their importance. They must have an unending source of fire, and a compelling and desired destination in mind in order to bring forth the change they seek to achieve. They must be able to confront and conquer an onslaught of resisting forces, dedicated to protecting the status quo.

Can you think of anything right now in your organization or your personal life, which you are totally committed to making better?

Competence

It is foolish to tackle something and not know what you are getting involved with. On occasion you may blindly fall into something grand, but the people who are most successful in introducing new innovations and improvements have devoted a great deal of time and energy to understanding the important issues and their implications.

We will examine competence from the perspective of the attributes of expertise and experience. Great challengers are knowledgeable about their subject. They observe it, read about it, and study it. They reflect on it and ask tough questions about it. In addition, they get actively involved and learn even more by doing. Laird Hamilton could not learn about staying on a surfboard just from extensive reading about the breaking motion of waves or the principles of balance. He had to spend countless hours in the ocean, where he developed his talents through experiencing a diversity of waves, and some particularly nasty wipe-outs. Lisa Allgood's past experience in working for Merck, the pharmaceutical giant, enabled her to more fully understand the issues and the value that AstraZeneca brought to the table in creating Prilosec OTC.

If there is something you are committed to building or changing, ask yourself now: are you willing to develop the competence necessary to make it happen?

Self-assurance

Have you ever doubted yourself? Even if you are passionate about something, have a driving vision and the necessary capabilities to pull it off, you can still get stuck in neutral and avoid taking action. Self-assurance will be explored through two important internal factors, self-confidence and courage.

Confidence is the subtle but essential force that enables you to take the courageous steps toward growth. Commitment and competence build confidence. And that belief in yourself is the key that is needed to unlock the door to your courage.

Ultimately it does take courage to stand up and act for what you believe in, especially when facing opposition. Leaders understand the saying that "adversity doesn't build character, it reveals it." When you decide to challenge the way things have always been done, you will indeed face some adversity. The strength of your courage and depth of your convictions will then be tested.

People who successfully challenge the way things are done show courage in a couple of important ways. First, they take action when the outcome is unknown—and there is plenty of unknown or uncertainty when taking risks necessary to grow. Second, they persevere in spite of constant and sometimes severe criticism. Would you be willing to take a company public by defying the traditional, almost sacred channels of submitting to Wall Street investment firms? Larry Page and Sergey Brin of Google did. Would you be able to keep the faith when thousands of people started bashing your efforts, on websites devoted to removing you from your job? Welcome to the world of Chris Bangle, who daily faces public criticism and ridicule such as:

"I think Bangle has the designing capabilities of a six-year old. A front view of the new BMW's look all right but when you look at them in 3d they look like cheap Japanese cars. Hey, Chris you'll fit right in at Pontiac or Ford, not here. You are ruining BMW."

"I ran to buy my current e46 sedan in 2005 right after I saw the pictures of new 2006 ugly beast. Despite technological advances of the car it looks so ugly I can't imagine owning one."

"I was planning on buying a 3 series last year until I saw how ugly the new models looked. Please rethink this ridiculous new design."

In the face of this onslaught, Bangle has persevered and remains devoted to the new, different designs. By the way, these designs have brought significant increases in the BMW market share. So much for Bangle's move to Pontiac.

It is certainly easy to see the relationship between commitment and courage. Would you take the great risks associated with acting courageously, if you were not totally invested in the outcome? Having competence also helps, as expertise and experience forge the confidence that is needed to try something that has never been attempted before.

Each of the three primary attributes is comprised of two related attributes, which will be examined in later chapters. In addition to providing relevant examples and practical information, we will add several reflection questions, asking you to think about what you are reading and how it relates to you. We hope you will take time to thoughtfully reflect on these questions.

There is also a summary chapter for each of the three primary attributes, where actions are offered on how individuals and organizational leaders can strengthen or build these attributes.

We have included three additional chapters that we believe will also offer valuable help and guidance. The first is a discussion on the subject of maturity, and its relationship to successful change and growth challenges. We have also included a section on how the ideas and lessons in this book can be applied in helping an organization stimulate sustainable growth. The final chapter is a review and summary of the key lessons.

Change is in our DNA; however, not every physical change is determined by our genes. Each of us can influence to some degree how we look or how we behave. When you tackle difficult goals such as trying to permanently drop an extra 10 pounds, tighten up the abs or be more effective in handling conflict with other people, you know how tough it is to change the ways you have done things for years. Our guess is you can immediately relate to the importance of commitment, competence and self-assurance in these personal challenges. You will find them to be valuable assets in whatever challenges you face.

As you read about what it takes to challenge, change and produce growth, you will recognize that the focus will be primarily on the human attributes. We know that organizational growth today often requires great technology, effective systems, financial capital, and a risk-accepting culture, yet the key element is people who are able and willing to tackle the challenge of growth. Great ideas come from the human imagination, much more so than from flashy technology or deep pockets. And the world is chock-full of people who, capitalizing on these attributes, have somehow figured out how to overcome the adversity of inadequate physical, financial, or technological resources to achieve remarkable success. *When it comes to growth, internal character trumps process, resources, and execution.*

We suspect that you have been bombarded with change. You know it is rampant, tumultuous, hard to manage, and a source of enormous confusion and frustration. You also know that change is essential for growth and breakthroughs. Those outcomes can never occur by continuing to do things in the same fashion.

We encourage you to reflect for a moment on what you believe needs to be done differently in your organization or business unit. It might be a compelling challenge of how to grow your business, increase volunteer support or funding for a special cause, or to greatly improve the way some process works. It need not be as spectacular as a 70-foot wave, but for you this challenge must be personally meaningful and important. Truthfully question yourself about whether you have what it takes to successfully bring about the desired growth *(see Figure 1)* you so much want to happen. Take advantage of these opportunities. They will point you toward the changes that must happen to strengthen your quest to challenge, change, grow and improve your piece of the world.

Figure 1: The Growth Formula

Growth occurs when people conceive and follow through on new ideas, requiring experimenting, tinkering, launching, and expanding. Within organizations, many assets and resources (such as technology, and capital, when aligned with the work that people do, leverage or accelerate growth.

Yet real growth is often thwarted for several reasons. The lack of resources can squash the energy for generating new ideas and impede growth. Also, the lack of commitment, competence and self-assurance can stop growth. When these attributes are lacking, people will show little or no interest, capabilities, or belief in themselves to do the work that must be done to achieve sustainable growth. Unfortunately, you cannot overcome the lack of these primary attributes by emphasizing the need to think outside the box, challenge more, take more risks, push back and other "must do" behaviors.

Conventional wisdom suggests that innovations or breakthroughs will most likely come when people are in an environment of abundant support systems and helpful resources. Assuming there are ideas to pursue, that is probably true. But growth ideas ultimately originate from people. In its early days, Southwest Airlines was forced to sell one of their four planes to make payroll. Would a disgruntled, non-committed, non-courageous group of people have created their now legendary 20-minute gate turnaround, which allowed them to continue offering a full flight schedule? And is Starbuck's coffee really that different from many other fine blends? How much of its spectacular success might be a result of CEO Howard Schultz's passion and vision of a completely different coffee-drinking experience? We can come up with countless examples of growth ideas that blossomed because of the internal character of people rather than the external assets of their surrounding environments.

Business managers know that it is like pulling teeth to generate growth opportunities working with people who lack commitment, competence or self-assurance. A pervasive lack of these three internal characteristics, even with an abundance of resources and a risk-accepting culture, will keep your dreams of growth from ever getting off the ground.

Chapter 3: Growth Requires Exploring the Unknown

Over the years, we have worked with numerous managers through leadership seminars, coaching, strategic planning and team development activities. We watch their progress and monitor why certain individuals can grow their business and why others struggle to achieve sales plans. During our early contact with managers, it becomes apparent who will make the behavioral adjustments to move their business units forward. These leaders understand that internal character is the catalyst for generating the climate for personal and business success.

You might wonder why anyone would need a catalyst for growth. Isn't it obvious that people and organizations need to grow in order to survive? Just because it is obvious does not mean it is easily accomplished. In fact, a natural force works against the willingness to grow. That force is comfort.

The Life Zones

In their daily lives, most people have experiences in the three zones of *The Life Zones Model (see Figure 2A)*: the Comfort Zone, the Growth (or Learning) Zone and the Panic Zone.

Figure 2A

The Comfort Zone represents the status quo or the belief that life is meant to be routine. Comfort Zoners take the easy route and avoid fixing what is wrong. While in this zone, they have a sense of control, familiarity, predictability, perhaps even a feeling of mastery, and they like it. They play it safe by "tip-toeing through the tulips" and "staying between the lines."

People stuck in the comfort zone do not like the boat to be rocked. They are satisfied with the status quo and believe that there is no need to change what they do or how they work. They are seldom, if ever, on the edge of breakthrough thinking about growth. But as they bask in their comfort, they wake up one morning to a changed world. The refusal to transcend comfort, control and custom ushers in a harder life than expected. The Comfort Zone is void of growth. People here demonstrate no belief or desire for change, so growth is not even an option. They may still have passion, but if they are unwilling to move beyond this region, others will often view them as intellectually tired, living in a state of dullness, or unengaged. This zone represents a state of maintaining, so people become emotionally detached from the search for difference. It is hard to find hope or opportunities for a better tomorrow with people who reside in the Comfort Zone.

The true leaders reside in the Learning Zone. It is the place where exploration, innovation, improvement, risk-taking and growth are normal. It is the home for moving beyond yesterday, everyday. Challenging current norms occurs here. These residents work on growing and express their learning by taking new steps. There is some anxiety and apprehension, as growth requires risk. Yet people here willingly place themselves in situations where they have never been before.

Was Laird Hamilton content to stay surfing 20-foot waves the rest of his life? Was Chris Bangle thoroughly satisfied with a few minor, relatively unnoticeable tweaks of the BMW? Did Lisa Allgood decide to stay with a conventional and familiar approach to launching a new product? These role models were well into their learning zones, experimenting, taking risks and even failing. They understood that moving beyond the safe harbor of complete comfort was required for great innovation and growth, and they were willing to go there.

In our leadership work, we often encourage participants to move into the learning zone through experiential activities, such as a high ropes course—a series of challenging elements located 30 to 40 feet off the ground. When presented with this challenge some people immediately remark "no way" or "this is stupid." But something soon begins to happen, as they learn more about it. These emotional outbursts soon change to "I'm going to give it a go." Within minutes, they are ready to move out and take the first step. Slowly, fear and trepidation give way to confidence and exhilaration. After the experience, the same people who were skeptical at first, will be shouting about how their accomplishment on the ropes was one of the most rewarding things they have ever done.

People who value learning are not afraid of moving out into the unknown. They know that some uncomfortable time spent in the Learning Zone is the price to be paid in order to ultimately arrive at a better destination.

The Panic Zone is an area that people, sometimes unintentionally, work their way into, because they don't have the skills or self-confidence to succeed. One person's Panic Zone might occur when she is forced to speak in front of a large group. Another might experience it when he must confront a peer over a disagreement or justify a failure to senior management. Pressure to perform throws them into chaos and they do not know how to respond. This is the Panic Zone—known for high blood pressure, chaos, confusion, distress, dysfunction, disengagement, poor performance—and no growth.

Many people encounter the panic zone when pushing the edges of their learning zones. They simply push the learning envelope too far, or too fast. They venture onto the treacherous Black Diamond trail, and discover too late, that they cannot keep their balance on the steep, icy slopes. They experience the desperation of being in over their heads, perhaps after taking a huge promotion in responsibility long before they are ready, or while testifying in a televised and politically-charged Senate hearing, without proper coaching or experience. Anyone who pursues continual learning and growth will occasionally bump into the Panic Zone. If fact, the edge along the learning and panic zones is often ripe with novel, growth opportunities.

But the Panic Zone can also surface in a much different way. Any person or company that makes the decision to stay safely huddled in the Comfort Zone will find the Panic Zone blocking their way toward learning and growth *(see Figure 2B)*. This is the penalty for routine, complacency, and predictability.

People in this Panic Zone have done plenty of harvesting, but have spent no energy preparing the soil for future harvests. Their easy lives of comfort and routine have left them in despair when it comes to succeeding in the future. For example, we have seen this in product-oriented, transaction-based salespeople who refuse to believe their customers now demand needs-based, consultative relationships, and who are unwilling to develop those skills. They end up firmly planted in the Panic Zone, anxious, frustrated and struggling to survive. They do not realize that *they must endure the discomfort of growth to avoid the pain of panic.*

Figure 2B

The duration of time spent lingering in the Comfort Zone will determine the length and severity of the Panic Zone experience. The Learning Zone is out there, but the path to it may be a longer, more frightening tunnel than expected.

Think about the local church with a senior pastor who must be in control of all areas of the church—worship, administration, finances, etc. The pastor places restrictions on congregational growth because this decision will allow him to control every element of the church. After 25 years of maintaining this approach, the pastor experiences health problems and suddenly retires. Other members of the so-called church leadership team are not prepared or able to make key decisions, organize a stewardship campaign, direct a worship service or reach out to the community. (That is the pastor's job, not mine!) It has become a status-quo situation. To further complicate the future, a new pastor arrives 18 months later with a different view of church leadership. He is not control-oriented and expects the members to be actively engaged in every aspect of church life. To his dismay, he finds a congregation and culture, wandering aimlessly in the wilderness of the Comfort Zone, with little or no appetite for learning and change. Taking on new responsibilities to grow and change will not only be hard for them, but threatening as well. They will immediately confront the Panic Zone, with only a very dim light at the end of this tunnel.

The Growth Frontier

The Comfort, Growth and Panic Zones—primarily relate to individuals and their personal and professional growth. In completing innovation work with our clients, we have utilized another perspective, The Growth Frontier Model, to show how organizations experience profitable and lasting growth. This concept is not difficult to understand. In fact, it provides the "thinking basis" for how to generate incremental revenue.

Organizations also have a couple of zones, *Today's Business* and the *Growth Frontier* (see Figure 3). *Today's Business* is based on the current customers an organization deals with, familiar products offered, processes done well, and to some extent an environment that is comfortable and understood. The *Today's Business* arena might loosely be considered the organization's comfort zone. It is our center for retreat and control.

Figure 3

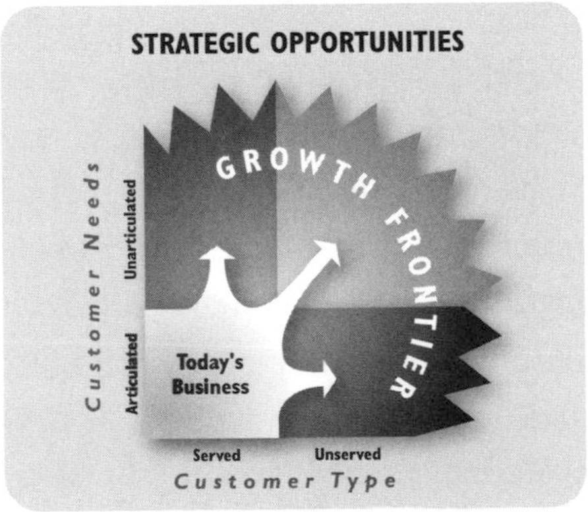

The future opportunities for organizations are found in the Growth Frontier. This area contains expanded business potential with current and new customers. It is also the arena where striking new products and services are brought forth, even before the needs for them have been articulated.

The Growth Frontier is a much different place. The frontier has opportunity—current customers with unarticulated and un-served needs; un-tapped customers whose needs are known and those whose needs are unknown. To explore the frontier, you must focus on the three quadrants outside of *Today's Business*. It is full of potential for business growth.

But, why do the vast majority of senior managers, middle managers, and sales professionals remain glued to *Today's Business*? The answer is simple. It provides a feeling of comfort, familiarity and security. Companies have the processes, resources and technology for developing new revenue streams, but they have difficulty moving people out of *Today's Business* into the *Frontier*. If individuals don't purposely venture out into the unknown frontiers of their own personal learning zones, innovation, risk-taking and growth will be hard to find in organizations.

Like individuals, organizations can also encounter a Panic Zone. This happens when they have not developed growth capabilities and are not prepared for a different world.

Consider the mortgage lending industry and how its growth has been affected by each zone. For the past decade, mortgage interest rates have been at historically low levels stimulating a national housing boom. During this period, mortgage loan originators (salespeople) lined their pockets with commission dollars due to record housing sales. Business was easy. Refinancing made their role similar to an order taker. Answer a telephone call, take a loan application, start the processing and wait to close the loan. It was the Comfort Zone with high personal rewards. Financial Service firms were also benefiting from the low-interest-rate environment. They became dependent on mortgage lending to boost company profit goals and achieve shareholder expectations.

By early 2005, interest rates moved to higher levels snuffing out the refinancing activity and creating a housing slump. The order takers were no longer experiencing heavy telephone activity. Many were clueless on how to develop loan activity. The Comfort Zone had lulled them into complacency. Easy had now turned to hard, resulting in originators and entire lending functions, falling swiftly out of the Comfort Zone into the Panic Zone. Financial service firms were no longer receiving large contributions to their bottom line from mortgage lending. In response to this turn of events, companies released low-producing loan originators to meet bottom-line objectives.

Some originators had been dwelling in the Learning Zone during the housing boom. They were working hard at developing relationships with real estate brokers and learning new technology. They knew the low interest rates would eventually dissipate, and mortgage lending would be left to the committed professionals. They and their organizations have continued to find success by carving out growth opportunities in the industry, because of their willingness to live in the Learning Zone.

Think about any company that has been in fortunate market conditions for some time and has come to believe that is the norm. When sales suddenly drop, stock price plunges downward, or they are threatened by a buyout, they virtually panic. Blue-chip talent starts bailing, command-and-control management replaces trust, stress levels climb, people quit treating each other with respect. We would define this as panic. Are these symptoms of your organization today? Remember, the blue skies of the opportunity-rich *Growth Frontier* that await you, can easily turn into the storm clouds of a threat-filled Panic Zone, if you remain confined in the comfort of *Today's Business* too long.

A Real Example of the Growth Frontier

Bill Struever is the CEO of the preeminent urban redevelopment firm, Struever Bros. Eccles & Rouse, headquartered in Baltimore, Maryland. Formed during the mid-1970's, the firm's initial office was located in his mother's basement. In Bill's words, "We even worked out a barter deal for room and board in return for fixing up my mom's new house." With over 350 professionals, SBER has been a major player in the restoration of the Baltimore waterfront and other landmark buildings. They are devoted to leading smart growth developments, creating unique live-work communities and 24-hour urban neighborhoods.

The firm hasn't always experienced bonafide success. Their initial project on the waterfront was a home purchased in 1976. Prior to this rehab assignment, Bill, Fred (his brother) and Cobber Eccles had been working on dollar homes (homesteading program). Bill's comment about their beginnings was, "We were working on dollar homes and wanted to do our own thing, and borrowed $10,000 from my mom to buy a house on the back side of Federal Hill. We fixed it up. And that was the beginning of our real estate business."

With Bill and Struever Bros., it has never been about *Today's Business*. More than 30 years later, SBER has 16 million square feet and nearly $5 billion of total investment in projects completed or under development. The firm's passion is more than transforming areas—it is transforming people by shifting old notions, breaking old habits, being true to commitments made to communities, and breathing new life into places that others didn't have the vision to transform. Urban Development experts have stated, "SBER has such a passion for these old buildings. They're not in communities to do one building. They see the bigger picture." Struever confirms, "What we love are edge neighborhoods that have tremendous untapped market potential. We just don't do suburban projects. It just doesn't bring joy to our heart and soul."

Bill expects all 350 employees to live in the Growth Zone. They work closely in a partnership effort to embrace the community's priorities. They take a prominent role in school partnerships to improve the quality of education for children. The firm teams up with community workforce programs to assist those in need to find skill-building roles with SBER. Struever has encouraged his people to be involved in volunteerism programs. For Struever and his firm, it is about transforming America's cities and being dedicated to changing things for the better. "We have a new way at looking at a neighborhood—one that sees not what it is, but what it can be."

SBER is able to expand its business because the people reside in the Learning Zone and the business focuses on the Growth Frontier. Through Bill Struever's leadership, the employees are committed to developing personally and contributing to the organization's growth. And the reward is that Struever Bros. Eccles & Rouse receives development opportunities that no other firm can imagine.

There is a word of caution about growth companies such as SBER.

Never forget that capitalizing on the Growth Frontier requires discipline and the commitment to build a comprehensive infrastructure. Without this backbone support, a company will move beyond its capacity to deliver on its promises and commitments. Customers will feel betrayed, employees will not be engaged and shareholders will not reap the rewards of revenue expansion. To sustain successful growth, companies must constantly scan their organizations, identifying and investing in the operational people and resources required to keep pace with expansion. They must be just as committed to implementing infrastructure and controls as designing marketing programs.

Final Comments

No doubt about it—growth is uncomfortable for people and organizations. And the desire and willingness for an individual to still pursue it, in spite of the difficulties and discomfort, comes from within. It comes from the character attributes that build commitment, competence and self-assurance. These attributes provide the real catalyst for people, individually and organizationally, to venture out into the sometimes treacherous, always unpredictable world of innovation and growth.

There Is No Box is intended to challenge you and your organization to develop the internal character necessary to dissolve the boundaries so that the Comfort Zone or *Today's Business* is not a defining reality in your life or company. Life is vibrant, significant and risky out in the Frontier, and living there is a way of life for the curious, the bold and the courageous, and ultimately the successful.

Our goal is to help you understand the attributes necessary to leave behind the status quo and to develop exciting, groundbreaking growth opportunities. We encourage you to step into your own Learning Zone, by reflecting deeply on what you are about to read, responding honestly to the thoughtful questions you will encounter, and challenging yourself to develop more possibilities for spurring growth.

The first stop will be the subject of commitment, where you will examine the two attributes that start it all, passion and vision.

PART 2: THE CHARACTER ATTRIBUTES OF GROWTH

"What lies behind us and what lies before us are small matters compared to what lies within us."

> — ***Ralph Waldo Emerson***, American essayist, philosopher and poet (1803-1882)

COMMITMENT

We have learned something over the years. You cannot simply will someone to be committed to a goal, principle or value. You cannot force them to become terribly excited or make them willingly put themselves at risk. Why do you think it is so hard to get some people to think or work "outside the box," or to take the risk of trying to grow their business in innovative, but unproven ways? Sometimes the desired outcomes are not meaningful enough for them to put forth the required effort. Many times they simply face so many roadblocks, that the feeling of hopelessness eliminates the energy to try.

We have also learned that when people are committed, they are engaged and energized, and will attempt extraordinary things even when there is more than a reasonable chance of falling short. Commitment is indeed a powerful force.

Commitment is comprised of passion and vision. Passion is that strong, emotional feeling about a belief. It requires the heart and the nervous system, not just the head. It provides a continuing, renewable source of energy. Taking on the status quo and taking stands on new ideas requires constant energy. It is hard and draining work. Think about something that you are working on that simply makes sense to do, compared to something which you have real passion about. You can feel the difference.

Vision is the clear mental picture of a destination or outcome that you desperately want to reach. Leadership guru Warren Bennis calls vision a "target that beckons." It is like a giant magnet that pulls an individual out of bed each morning, much like a trip to Disney World might do for an eight-year old. Vision brings clarity of purpose, allowing you to focus or channel your passion on a tangible, desired future.

Can one person's passion and vision change the world? Consider this. In 1988, LensCrafters associate Susan Knobler suggested that the company should serve a greater purpose by providing people in need with the opportunity to see more clearly. The idea was not about simply writing a check from a foundation. It was about having company associates, in a personal, hands-on way, become directly involved with those in need, by providing them with eye exams and glasses. This was a belief that Susan held deep in her heart. It did not take long to discover that a lot of other people, inside and outside of the company, shared her passion as well. Their collective dream of providing the "Gift of Sight" soon began and has since accomplished more than any of them could have possibly imagined—and on a world-wide scale.

In the first five years, they served 10,000 people. By the end of 2005, over 4 million grateful people had received the "Gift of Sight" from the caring associates of Luxottica Retail (the parent company of LensCrafters). By way of monthly optical missions cosponsored with Lions Clubs International, store associates and affiliated doctors deliver free vision screenings, eye exams and new or recycled glasses to more than 300,000 people in developing countries around the world, and another 400,000 in the United States and Canada, each year.

All of this because people became committed to making the world a better place, especially for those in need.

There are two important messages you should glean from this remarkable example. First, this is not easy work. Without even considering the mind-boggling challenges of logistics and organization, fulfilling a mission requires people to travel and set up shop in some remote and uncomfortable settings, work very long days, and deal with unforeseen problems. And they absolutely love it! For most, work on a mission is one of their most treasured life experiences. In fact, many at

Luxottica would tell you there is as much benefit to themselves, the givers, as to the recipients. Strong commitment has that effect on people.

Another message to take away is about how passion and vision can fuel growth. Most organizations would love to have the growth trajectory that Gift of Sight has experienced. But, keep in mind that it takes a tremendous amount of commitment and resources for Gift of Sight to serve hundreds of thousands of people each year. It also takes a healthy dose of creativity, innovation and risk taking. Over the years, those associated with Gift of Sight have constantly figured out new and better ways to collect glasses, provide eye exams, raise money, and work through the thousands of other challenges required to make their dream a reality. That devotion to innovation and change is what it takes to grow in any industry, and applies equally to for-profit businesses and non-profit endeavors.

You will find that the two attributes comprising commitment touch all of the other character attributes for growth. How many people do you imagine will step up to the extremely taxing work of growth if they really do not care? Will they display courage and perseverance when it is needed? Will they suffer through the discomfort of mistakes made when attempting to learn and apply new skills? Will they feel confident to step into the wilds of the growth frontier, if they are wavering in passion or question the intrinsic value of their destination? No, they won't. That is why without commitment, the other attributes essential for challenge and growth will remain guarded or concealed.

In the following two chapters, we will explore the subjects of passion and vision. You will be invited to reflect on the things about which you are deeply passionate and challenged to think about the future you would like to create, whether that future is for your family, your neighborhood, your work organization, or the world.

So open your mind and your heart. Think carefully about what you are reading and how it directly applies to you. Be willing to look deep inside yourself, so you can discover—or become more closely acquainted with—what you truly feel committed to. Then don't be surprised when fresh ideas for growth start surfacing much more frequently, and you feel a renewed sense of energy to pursue them.

Remember that improvement and growth do not just naturally happen on their own. They take work—the kind of work that can only come from commitment.

Chapter 4: A Fire in the Heart: Passion

"Look at the passion that she demonstrates in her work. He is so passionate about his family. You can see the passion in his eyes as he approaches gameday! Her passion about teaching children comes across in the classroom. He lacks the passion to make the changes needed to become a more effective leader. Where is the passion?"

It seems like the word *passion* is certainly receiving a lot of attention today. Why is this? Why is this emotion so critical to a person's success? And, why is this state vital for risk-taking and innovation?

Deep passion influences a person's behavior and engenders courage and a strong, emotional commitment.

Passion is difficult to describe, and yet, you know it when you see it. Watching Tiger Woods hit the golf ball, Kobe Bryant play basketball, Suze Ormond speak at financial seminars, Billy Graham preach at crusades, Steve Jobs promote the iPod®, and Picabo Street ski down a Black Diamond, you will understand what passion is. Passion is a force to be reckoned with. Without it, you experience the ordinary—the history professor with the same syllabus for the past 40 years or the plumber who promises but doesn't follow-through. Passion calls us to action and commitment. It moves us to be bigger and better than we ever thought possible. It provides the impetus for growth in individuals and companies.

Senior managers generally agree that their employees rarely challenge processes and take the risks necessary for growth. A major reason for this lack of risk-taking is the absence of personal passion and enthusiasm for their work. They are dispassionate about the company and its products, and often fail to see the passion, excitement and enthusiasm in their leaders. They don't see new ideas, innovations and improvements taking place, or a real sense of urgency to change things. The passion for moving to something new is not registering with employees because their managers are promoting the status quo, even when demanding outrageous revenue growth which simply cannot be achieved by continuing to do things the same old way. Why is this? Do these managers fail to understand the connection between passion and growth?

Passion Is a Force

Passion makes people do strange things. Anything having to do with the "heart and soul" will engage people wildly. Passion shoots straight from the heart. It is about being in love. And when you are in love, the soul wants the heart to be involved as well. This combination—heart and soul—will have a significant influence on a person's behavior, focus and interests. It creates the energy and drive to move people in different ways.

Just ask Greg Allgood about passion doing strange things to people. Greg's career at Procter & Gamble (P&G) was hitting its stride. He played a significant role in the development of olestra, a fat substitute, and led efforts to share olestra's safety and potential public health benefit with the scientific community. Allgood remembers: "The most important opportunity surfaced when I had a face off on Oprah with olestra's most vocal critic. I prepared well for that meeting. But, when the face off started, all the preparation gave way to my passion for the potential public benefit of this new technology. I wanted to win this debate. It was important to the product, to P&G, and to me."

This passion later led Greg into a new role and career direction at P&G—Entrepreneur and Missionary for Safe Drinking Water. After a brief detour leading P&G's external alliance work in nutritional products, Allgood became part of the team focused on providing safe drinking water for the developing world. As part of this team, he experienced first-hand the unhealthy, inhumane situations, young third world children were living in. These images drove Greg to his vision that P&G could play an important role in addressing this crisis that kills 4,000 children a day. Things were going well until P&G couldn't make a commercial success out of the venture. However, sustained by his passion, and similar to how LensCrafters (Luxottica) had embarked on the Gift of Sight program, Allgood envisioned that P&G would adopt safe drinking water as it's focal program for corporate philanthropy.

As this strategy unfolded, Greg had his defenders and detractors—as expected. His energy, fueled by his unrelenting passion for helpless children, allowed him to take on detractors—some who were senior leaders at P&G. Passion was Greg's impetus for overcoming several crisis points where the program was to be shelved. The project failed many times before it became successful. Greg simply wouldn't give up and found a path, never explored in P&G's 172-year history, to expand the program. This meant risking his career, but to Greg it seemed a small price to pay for saving children's lives.

Support and encouragement eventually came from the current CEO, A. G. Lafley, as well as three past CEOs, and Greg was chosen to lead P&G's focal philanthropy program, the Children's Safe Drinking Water program. It took Greg's passion and limitless energy to explain the broad benefits that P&G would receive by adopting this cause. By building a broad network of support both within and external to P&G, the program became active in more than a dozen countries in the developing world and delivered more than 500 million liters of safe drinking water in the first three years.

Passion took Greg Allgood down a career path he could not have foreseen. Passion for the vision was the motivating force to change the lives of unfortunate children. His ability to "light fires" in certain corridors at P&G enabled the giving of safe drinking water to millions of children worldwide. But we do know that without it, companies and their employees are in danger of winding up in a place called Nowhere.

Passion and Its Impact

Not everyone possesses passion. In fact, fewer people seem to have a "True North" in their lives. Most people are just driving to work everyday and going through the motions. They have emotionally checked out. If their heart is engaged in something, it is not their work. The tangible offshoots of passion—drivers such as innovation, creativity and imagination—do not seem to be the heart and soul of the American workforce.

Just look at the *Characteristics of Admired Leaders* research, developed by Jim Kouzes and Barry Posner. Since 1988, thousands of prospective leaders have completed this survey where they have selected seven characteristics from a list of 20 leadership attributes. *Caring* and *Imaginative* are two characteristics being assessed. Over the years, these two characteristics have been selected by only about 20 percent of the respondents. People do not look for these attributes in their leaders nearly as frequently as they do other characteristics, especially honest, competent, and forward-looking. So, do our leaders lack passion? Are they the source of this "heart and soul deficiency" at work?

*   *   *   *   *

At Ditmas Middle School in Brooklyn, NY, there is no heart-and-soul deficiency. Nancy Brogan, the principal, leads daily with passion. Her school consists of about 1,300 kids, of which 90 percent are at or below the poverty level. She has kids from 48 different countries, who speak 39 different languages. She even has students who at ages 10 to 13 can't read or write in any language. And in a typical year, about 480 kids leave the school and 500 enter. Does this sound like your ideal job situation?

Nancy's job responsibilities included staffing, curriculum, parental involvement, discipline and keeping kids in school, but Nancy also decided to attack how public education was delivered and funded.

She "pounded the pavement" to get her hands on computer money. With support from J.P. Morgan Chase, Nancy arranged that every student in her school would receive a personal computer at home free of charge. Chase anted up nearly $4.5 million to provide computers—and desks—for all 1,300 students. Not to be left out, all members of the Ditmas staff—including the custodians—received a computer. It was total participation and commitment.

Nancy Brogan was passionate about educating children. She believed that her kids (and kids everywhere) should be afforded every opportunity to be educated. She was relentless in the pursuit of better education for her kids. Since her passion was about education, not just figuring out how to get computers, Nancy did something very unconventional. In order for the children to keep the computers, their parents had to come to Ditmas for a three-hour tutorial on operating a computer. Through this action, Nancy created an innovative way to keep parents more involved in the education process of their children.

There was one other caveat: in order for the kids to keep the computers, they had to stay in school. Nancy was determined to do what she could to prevent them from ever dropping out of school. If it meant finding a way to provide computers and involve parents, then so be it.

Providing computers to the students delivered several positive results. The number of kids leaving Ditmas dropped, as did the number of occurrences requiring disciplinary action. And of course the kids found new ways to use the computers to improve their learning.

The passion that enveloped Nancy Brogan could be described as: an extreme or inordinate desire; or boundless enthusiasm. Curt Rosengren, a passion catalyst, says that passion is the energy that comes from bringing more of you into what you do. Passion is about strong, emotional feelings. It requires the heart and the soul, not just the mind. Passion is a deep and positive emotion. It is usually easy to spot, because people cannot help but visibly act on things about which they are passionate.

Passion is evident by the great talent it attracts. Organizations with heart and soul rarely have to recruit. People come to them. The environment encompasses them. They sprint toward their dream. Passion is the great magnetic force which pulls people irresistibly to it. Walk the halls of your company or business unit. Are you proud about the talent wandering around? Do you hear people "raising the walls" about their work? Do you hear people talking about the new waterfront they are building? Are people excited about the contributions they are making to their customer's future? Does passion resonate throughout the organization? Do you truly believe that the target is attainable?

Passion promotes and produces mistakes. Chris Bangle, the former

Chief design officer for BMW, looked at design as an art. His team would envision numerous designs and create many drawings before embracing a design. Their passion flowed from their inner being. It moved them to search for the painting that is lodged in the soul. It was hard for them to see until it was being shaped. Through many starts and restarts, the car would come alive. It did not happen on the first try. It took perseverance driven by passion. The mistakes would mount up, the criticisms reach a feverish pitch and the costs begin to escalate. Arrows would be flying from all directions—automotive media, dealerships, the boardroom, engineering, etc. Some of the mistakes were stupid. But, ultimately they produced the "new strokes" that moved the design into the winning column. By the mid 2000's, Bangle's passion for design had allowed BMW to forge ahead of Lexus and Mercedes in the U.S. sales race.

Passion fuels courage. And courage is vital for challenging the process. History has given the world many passionate leaders. Consider Jesus, Gandhi, Martin Luther King, Mother Teresa and Abraham Lincoln. Their lives were marked by courageous acts fomented by their beliefs. People with beliefs act out of the passion they feel for those beliefs. Without the passion for civil rights, Martin Luther King would not have faced off with George Wallace. His courage allowed him to stand-up for the rights of minorities, the poor and down-trodden knowing that jail could be a part of his future. Abraham Lincoln had great love for the country and its people. This bountiful love gave Lincoln the courage even in dark days to stand up against the evil of slavery. Jesus' compassion fueled his ministry of healing and love for the sick and the poor. He struggled with the authorities because his actions were creating a new view of the law. Ultimately, Jesus had the courage to give up His life for the mission.

Think about it. These leaders have been gone for years, but their lives and their work remain the topic of every day life. Interestingly, it is not about wealth or fame. It starts with the passion for their mission. Is the passion for the company's mission creating acts of courage in your organization?

Arousing Passion in Organizations

Does your organization have passion? We have worked with enough senior leaders and their teams to know that passion is a scarce commodity in corporate America today. The passion is missing. The hallways are void of energy. We are just not hearing employees "screaming to high heaven" over their work. Employees are not saying:

> *"I love my job! The work that I'm doing makes me want to jump out of bed every morning and get after it. It gives me a sense of purpose for my life. I can see every day that I make a difference for the company, my family and myself."*

In companies today, too many people have sealed up their hearts and the passion is not flowing. There is just no life. Passion needs to be ratcheted up to new levels.

To bring companies out of their slumber, leaders must spend time listening and observing, looking for passion, digging it up, and extolling it. They must search their hearts and souls and find what resides deep in their hearts. The passionate leaders become aware of their dreams, desires and beliefs. It becomes the foundation for their life. They listen actively to those dreams, desires and beliefs. Small steps are taken to move the dream forward. It extends into the business. The leader's passion moves the small wins along. Growth happens. People see major victories as the small wins mount up. But, for the leader, the dream is still just as important as the results. The voice of passion rallies each and every employee to sustain the momentum. The flames have engulfed the organization. The hallways are now stirred up. People are dancing. They have the swagger because the passion has enveloped them. The internal fire moves people to think more, work harder and throw caution to the wind. They are committed.

How did this all start? The leader looked inside and agreed to a complete excavation. By digging, he found out what was moving him. The internal Bunsen Burner had not been turned off. There was indeed a flame burning, fueled by the passion, that although hidden deep, was there.

How can we ask people to challenge the conventional norms if there is no flame or it has no fuel? An organization promotes risk-taking through the passion of its leaders. It is that internal flame that creates external growth opportunities. When leaders find a way to discover and unleash that passion in themselves, and others, real growth has a chance. The buried treasure of passion needs to be found and unearthed. Because it is sometimes well hidden, we must work diligently to surface it.

So, if passion is vital for innovation and growth to occur, how do leaders cultivate it in themselves and their companies? Consider the following possibilities for yourself:

- *Understand what excites you in your work.* Every morning the fire inside of you should ignite. It should propel you into the day and provide impetus for your daily activities. For the next month, grab a journal and end your day by writing about the inspiring aspects of it. What activities charged you up? Which projects are providing stimulating growth? What work is always intriguing to you? What subjects do you enjoy reading about? After 30 days, look at the patterns. What conclusions can you draw from this data? Are you working on projects that matter and have meaning? Is your work stimulating passion?

- *Become more effective at sharing the company's vision with your associates.* An inspiring vision is the leader's primary tool for developing passion in the workplace. Leaders need to accept the responsibility of creating a vision and communicating it to all employees. Generate some excitement and enthusiasm in the organization by giving people a compelling view of the future. Vision can stir up people's passion. The future is an important and exciting subject. Stir up passion.

- *Make your message memorable.* Employees want to hear their leader's commitment to the company's products, services and future. Passionate communications separates the "great leaders" from the "good leaders." Without a passionate voice, a leader will fail to motivate, inspire and electrify the troops. And the company will languish and not achieve its growth objectives. In fact, great leaders do not talk about creating more wealth and developing more capitalists. Instead, they focus on building rapport by connecting with their people through their personal stories, daily adventures and anecdotes. Share the stories about customer meetings and experiences that have raised your passion level. Let people know why you are in love with the company.

Howard Schultz, CEO and founder of Starbucks, is the example of "being out there with passion." In a recent *U.S. News & World Report*, it was stated that "he's not the stereotypical cheerleader, but Schultz, who visits 30 to 40 Starbucks stores a week, believes that a corporate leader must share unbridled enthusiasm with his employees. "I need to touch as many people as possible — I want to spend time with people," he says. "That's the single most important thing I'm doing." His enthusiasm and energy is one of the reasons why the people behind the counter in the stores are friendly and passionate. Have you seen the CEO from your bank at the local branch lately? The absence of passion for the branch employees, the customer and the business should provide you some valuable information about their interest in your long-term financial success.

- *Approach your work with passion and enthusiasm.* Keep in mind that you are a model for each employee. Your exuberance can give them encouragement. This encouragement can be a catalyst for developing passion in people. Leaders must view their office as the enemy and the frontline meeting rooms as your ally. Any way that leaders can promote energy and excitement will be a driving force in developing the business.

- *Talk about the importance of passion in the company.* Let employees know that this emotion is important to developing new ideas and building revenue. Explore the strategy of allocating a certain percentage of employee time to idea-generation. Consider assessing each employee's contribution to idea development in the annual performance review. Allocate a portion of the annual compensation plan to rewarding new ideas.

Self-Awareness—Your Passion Formula

It is time to stop reading and start thinking—about your own passion. Take a moment and reflect on the following questions. They will help you discover what really moves you, and the kinds of risky challenges you would be willing to tackle.

- What is it that gets your engine started everyday? What activities, assignments or projects motivate you into exemplary performance? What do you find virtually impossible to set aside?
- How does your work involve your passion?
- Does the passion level need to be raised in your life? How will you accomplish this?

Leader Awareness—Raising the Passion Level In The Organization

The top leaders in the company need to be engaged around creating a "passion-filled" environment. Describe your company's environment today. As a leader, are you satisfied/dissatisfied, encouraged/discouraged with the excitement and exuberance in the organization's environment? Write about your answer and discuss it with the other leaders.

- As a leader, what actions are you planning on taking to raise the decibel level in your organization? It is your responsibility to "grow the company." And passionate, energized environments are critical to revenue growth. So, what are you going to do? How will you implement your plan? Most importantly, when will you move forward?
- How will your boss, direct reports, board members and others assess your contribution to creating a passionate, energized work environment? Are you excited about the company and your work or do you have a cynical view of the future? As a leader, in what ways must you ignite your passion to accelerate a "growth envi-

ronment?"

- Finally, what systems can you implement to sustain a passion-filled environment?

Chapter 5: A Better Place to Be: Vision

On October 4, 2004, SpaceShipOne rocketed into history, becoming the first private manned spacecraft to exceed an altitude of 328,000 feet twice within the span of a 14-day period, and claiming the $10-million Ansari X-Prize. SpaceShipOne and its airborne launcher, White Knight, was considered at that moment to be the most promising widely recyclable and efficient uses of advanced aerospace technology seen in recent years.

The man who spearheaded a great deal of this winning effort was Burt Rutan. It was his company, Scaled Composites, that designed and created this breakthrough space vehicle. Burt had been associated with aeronautical breakthroughs most of his life, leading the way in the development of strong, yet lightweight aircraft built from composite materials. Perhaps you may have heard about one of his other designs. In 1986, the world got a glimpse of Voyager. With an airframe weight of only 939 pounds, Voyager was the first aircraft to fly completely around the world non-stop, and without refueling.

Winning the X Prize may be just the beginning for Rutan and his pilots. Around the time of his breakthrough flight in late 2004, Rutan remarked,

"I absolutely have to develop a space tourism system that is at least 100 times safer than anything that has flown man into space, and probably significantly more than that."

Did he say space tourism system?

With the exception of a couple of very wealthy passengers hitchhiking on a flight with the Russians, space travel had always been the domain of NASA or governments from other countries. Burt Rutan was looking at definitely changing the rules of the game. He had a vision of an exciting, new opportunity for people to visit space. By challenging the government's monopoly on developing and building space ships, his dream has been to take the commercial travel business into space with a private company (not a government agency) leading the charge. As Rutan has noted, "Within the next 10 to 12 years, hundreds of thousands of people will be taking trips into space. And they will be paying $100,000 to go on this journey."

Do you think his vision seems a little far-fetched? Time will tell how successful Burt and his fellow challengers are in making their dreams come true. But one thing Burt and others like him have taught us. Changing the way things are and creating breakthroughs require vision, along with a healthy dose of passion.

In fact, vision is often fueled by unending passion, as we believe was the case with Burt Rutan. Since he was a young boy, he was a builder. He "loved" to design and construct model airplanes. As he once remarked, "I had this fascination about building model airplanes and always making them better." It was his joy to wake up and think about flying in space and building the rocket that would take him there. Even as a boy, he was already engaged in creating his vision of the future.

This fascination that took root as a boy blossomed into a passion as an adult. One of his greatest accomplishments was the revolutionary wing design that has allowed his rocket to glide back from space. In describing how the design was conceived, Rutan gave us a glimpse into the energy and creativity that passion produces. Taking the problem to bed with him (as passionate people are known to do), one night he jumped out of bed at 3:00 in the morning yelling—"I got it, I got it." His wife brought the drawing board into the bedroom and the design went down on a sheet of paper. Passion never sleeps. You live with it every minute of the day—and night.

We have come across many people who clearly indicated they had passion about something, but unlike Rutan, lacked enough disciplined focus to make any significant change. There are those who say they are extremely passionate about customer service, yet do little more than complain how much better it needs to be in their companies. Others claim to be totally committed to employee education and development. They will say it is a sin not to enable people in an organization to develop themselves fully. Yet they are not coming forth with any options that counteract the significant budget and time constraints that hamper ongoing education processes. People like these examples have passion and are genuinely well intentioned. They just often do not have a clear picture of the future they want to create, and consequently become frequently and frustratingly sidetracked in their efforts to lead the way for change.

Vision is a cornerstone of leadership. Even in a world of widely diverse and frequently disagreeing opinions, just about everyone who reads about, writes about, studies or teaches leadership agrees that to be a leader, one must have a vision of the future. Leaders must have a clear picture of what they are attempting to accomplish and the future destinations to which they are trying to take other people. And those great accomplishments and new destinations always require some kind of change.

Think about it. How inspiring would it have been in 1963, if while standing in front of thousands of hopeful people, Martin Luther King had proclaimed, "I have a dream—to keep everything in this nation exactly as it is today." Or how about John Kennedy, if he would have said, "Going to the moon or establishing the Peace Corps is for dreamers. My job is to not rock the boat." If we are not mistaken, even Jackie Kennedy had a vision about a much different looking White House, and was responsible for bringing about some very dramatic changes in its physical and symbolic appearance.

It is virtually impossible to bring about change, if you cannot clearly see what a successful end result can be. Without a dream of riding a mountainous wave, would Laird Hamilton have been inspired to be towed in behind a Jet Ski and conquer the unridden realm? With everything else on a principal's plate, would Nancy Brogan have devoted much time to begging for money, if she did not have a vision of a rewarding education for every poor child in the country? Simply speaking, vision drives change. Its power helps pull us around or through the inevitable obstacles that block our efforts to improve the way thing are done.

A few years back, Ben & Jerry's Ice Cream was on the verge of having to shut down, because the amount of their liquid waste was overwhelming the local community disposal system. Along came Gail Mayville, an administrative assistant not a Ph.D. in environmental chemistry, who concocted and implemented a rather novel solution. Because of her farming background, she believed that pigs might eat the half-diluted waste and "organically" recycle it. She kept calling farmers until she found a partner, and then she had to convince the ice cream company to buy the pigs for him. (Do you think that might have been seen as a bit of an unusual purchase request for an ice cream company?) Her idea worked and a huge problem was averted. When asked why she chose to take on that problem she replied she was driven by the legacy of leaving an environmentally sound planet for her children. Gail's vision about a clean world moved her to think beyond her "job description" and led to her direct involvement in other environmental innovations that benefited much more of the world beyond Ben & Jerry's.

More recently, Carly Fiorina, the former CEO of Hewlett Packard, had to defend the acquisition of Compaq Computer and herself against influential members of the HP Board and the powerful Packard family. Her successful defense and the ultimate approval by the HP shareholders of the Compaq acquisition can be partially attributed to her convincing vision of the combined company's future. In 2006, HP's results have been extraordinary.

Give some thought to your own examples of people who have had to face tough challenges in order to bring about great change or innovation. Did these people have some kind of vision or did they all just get lucky and fall into something better? Our experience tells us that people who are willing to step up and take on change indeed must have very compelling visions, dreams, outcomes, or whatever you prefer calling them. And they then channel their deep passion toward those ends they so desperately want to achieve.

One of the lessons learned from Gail Mayville is that vision trumps organizational position. You can indeed challenge the current norms and change the world without being the top dog. And from Carly Fiorina we have learned that creating change, especially big change, can be a nasty struggle even if you are the CEO. Position power is not enough to guarantee success. It takes passion and vision to persevere. (For CEO's, it also takes ongoing support from the board of directors, which Fiorina ultimately lost in early 2005.)

A second lesson learned from Gail Mayville is that people at all levels in the organization can have dreams about a better company or for that matter a better world (as she had). Is it even feasible that the answer your company needs to keep the doors open, or to leave your competitors in the dust, could be in one of their heads right now? You may want to give that some thought!

Can You Have A Vision

It would be accurate to say that most of the people with whom we have worked over the years do not consider themselves to be great visionaries. Not only have they constantly admitted their lack of competence in this, but in one of the leadership assessment instruments we have frequently used, scores measuring visioning activities are generally the lowest of all measured leadership behaviors. That is not really surprising. After all, in most cases the emphasis and effort placed on producing today's results far exceeds those placed on achieving tomorrow's. If for no other reason, people have simply not had enough experience with vision to feel very confident about it.

There are a couple of comments we would like to offer about this perception of visioning abilities. First, there is a big difference in being considered a visionary and having a powerful vision about something. Think about that for a moment. Can you see a difference?

We found it interesting that upon closer examination, so many of these self-proclaimed non-visionaries did in fact have vision. It may have been about the type of education they wanted for their children, an entirely new way to bring a new non-prescription pain relief to market, revitalizing their places of worship, or yes, even in making their work accomplishments better and more meaningful. Most of them did indeed have an important something in their lives that they were committed to and driving toward.

Secondly, we noticed that a large number of people when trying to make the case for their weakness as visionaries would remark how they were just unable to look out and see a future very clearly. They could not create a vivid picture of a different tomorrow, without feeling like they were taking a fantasy trip to La La Land. Looking into the future was a waste of time, because it was not real, like the present. Besides, why do it, since everything is going to change anyway before you get there!

Does any of this sound familiar to you?

But guess what. We have found that literally everyone has a greatly developed capability to look into the future and paint very detailed and precise scenarios about what might happen. And they do it quite frequently, sometimes everyday. However, this capability is most commonly referred to as worrying, not visioning, and a lot of people have become near experts at it.

Isn't it fascinating how skilled most of us can be at clearly envisioning a future that we don't want, vs. one that we do? For example, which do you hear more frequently, people commenting that they:

- Do not want to be downsized, or that they want to be indispensable to their companies.
- Do not want to take the time to do performance reviews, or they want to give their people every opportunity to be great.
- Do not want to hang around a company that does not seem to value employees, or they want to help make their company one of the best places in the area to work.

We have found the percentage of "don't want" remarks is far greater than the "do want's." People often feel they are victims of their environment, not owners of it.

Trailblazers who take on the status quo and are successful in creating a new way of doing or growing things have a vision of a future they want. They are defiantly dissatisfied with the way things currently are. Rather than merely lament about the disappointing present, they use that dissatisfaction to envision, develop and go after a more satisfying, desirable future. And they keep their eyes glued to the prize they are seeking.

Chris Bangle saw a distinctively differently looking BMW. Nancy Brogan saw a novel way of providing education to kids at one of the most crucial points in their lives. Did Chris and Nancy have plenty to worry about? No doubt. But they worried less about all the things that could be done to them, and instead devoted their energies on what could be done by them.

Remember, knowledge drives growth, and wealth comes from the human imagination.

Wealth is not just having more and more of the old things, but having new things. Those new things will always come from people who are willing to imagine possibilities that today do not exist, and then put forth the effort (and incur the risk) to make those visions become real.

The word *visionary* might imply that you are capable at looking ahead and imagining a much different future for just about any aspect of your life or the world. You do not have to have that skill in order to produce change. But you do need to have at least one thing of great importance in your life that you deeply want to become or accomplish. Clear destinations and stirring passion about reaching them will provide the emotional resolve and boundless energy you must have in order to figure out the best actions to take, and to overcome the resistance that blocks your way to groundbreaking growth.

Making a Difference

We came across an extraordinary example of what having a powerful and focused vision can do to produce remarkable change. One of the things we appreciated most about this example was how it made us step back and think differently about what a powerful or compelling vision really is, and how the context or circumstances are so important in finding meaning from the vision. Hopefully, it will cause you to reflect as well.

Ever heard of Bayview, VA? Probably not. It is a small, rural, poverty stricken community in eastern Virginia. Years back, most of the homes had but two rooms. And so you will know, one of them was not a bathroom, because indoor plumbing did not exist there. (Think about that for a moment.) Their water supply was from a small well, which was frequently contaminated by waste from the outhouses that were still common. The electrical wiring was old, dangerous, and not even close to code, resulting in un-preventable fires. Roofs leaked and the cracked walls and windows let the wind whip through with very little resistance. Do you see the picture?

But Bayview had one other thing, a resident named Alice Coles, who literally altered a virtually inevitable future for these impoverished and seemingly hopeless people. Through Alice's leadership, this community developed and got behind a vision of something beyond their wildest dreams. Now brace yourselves because you may not believe what you are about to read! Their vision was *to move across the street*.

To move across the street was not a metaphor or a spiritual revelation. Their dream was to find a way to tear down some of the old buildings that were across the road from their dilapidated dwellings, build a new block of livable homes, and move into them. That was it—that was the dream.

They were not dreaming of a vacation home in the mountains, a cabin on the lake, or even the condo on the golf course. No, all they longed for was a place to stay warm and dry, and that had running water—indoors. And for them that dream seemed as impossible as growing younger might be for the rest of us.

Today Alice's neighbors and friends live on the other side of the street—in modern new homes, complete with indoor plumbing, thermostat-controlled comfort and family-centered front porches. Because of Alice's relentless pursuit of a better world for her community, an impossible dream became a reality for all of them. Her vision made a difference for Bayview, VA.

When people think of grand visions, many examples come to mind. We have already mentioned King's "I have a Dream" which may be the most notable, and Kennedy's mission to the moon. Gandhi's relentless pursuit of freedom for India, and Ronald Reagan's vision of a Berlin (and world) without a wall are other examples of bold, ambitious dreams. Along with these, our list will now include Alice Cole's desire to simply help her friends and neighbors move across the street.

Let us offer one final thought before you start examining the extent that you have a compelling vision that is calling you to action. We have found that people sometimes look for vision in the wrong place. That is, they try to see a future only in their head, but fail to seek it in their hearts. Remember this. You must be emotionally charged about a vision for it to inspire you to take on and change the seemingly impenetrable forces of the status quo. You must feel strongly attached to and deeply convinced in your heart about a vision. You must really want it. You must be firmly determined to make it a success. If your inner voice is only saying things like "this vision makes sense," or "it would be nice if it came to pass," you are likely doomed. Those are messages solely from your head and they are not enough. Many times the extraordinary things that people have pursued and accomplished would never have even been attempted, if the sole determinant was logic based on the current ways of doing things. Thank goodness there have been those who listened to their hearts, defied conventional wisdom, and helped change the world.

Strengthening Your Vision

One of the ingredients that champions of growth possess is vision. Leading change and achieving growth is tough work, so you need to know what you want to become and why it is important. Now it is time for you to spend some time reflecting on the degree that you have a clear end in mind, a vision for something of great importance for you. Don't look to find something that you feel you *should* be committed to achieving. Find the destinations you are committed to achieving. That is the real source of energy, creativity and perseverance you need to break free from the strong gravitational pull of "how things are done around here."

Be aware that finding the destination may take some soul searching. Also, understand that you might come up feeling empty, when you are unable to discover what you want to devote yourself to. Whether due to fatigue, being dreadfully overwhelmed or the lack of confidence that you can impact change, you may find it safer to hold back and not put your heart and soul into a career, an idea, or a person.

But we encourage you to keep looking. Pursuing your own special dreams, vs. tagging along on everyone else's will bring a whole new sense of purpose and meaning to your life. And who knows, you just might make your piece of the world a much better place for you and many other people.

Getting Started

For a few minutes, sit back and let your mind imagine what the world might become a few years from now. Have some fun with this. For example, how could cars be different, or computers, movie theaters, amusement parks, vacations or customer service? Just let your mind wander into areas that would really be worthwhile, or just plain cool if they occurred. Be daring and jot down your ramblings.

Now think back on some ideas about which you have passion or consider deeply important to you. These might include family, work goals, something to do with your religious or spiritual life, a social or charitable cause, a hobby, or anything else. What are the things in your life that truly light you up?

There is a big difference between searching for something to do and searching for something to create or achieve. Can you think of at least one thing that you really want to change, make happen or accomplish, in any part of your life—something that would provide you enormous satisfaction or fulfillment.

How much passion do you have for it? On a scale of 1 to 10 (low to high), how bad do you want it? (If it is not at least in the 7 to 8 range, you probably need to keep searching.)

Had you asked Alice Coles, a few years ago what she most wanted to see in the future, she may have said something like, "every single person in my community living in a decent home." The guys at Google may have responded to the same question with, "The perfect search engine. No matter what search words you type in, you will be immediately directed to the exact information you are looking for."

How would you answer that question about your passion? That is, what do you most want to see in the future? Describe it. Make it as clear and recognizable to others as you can. (And don't worry if it sounds a bit "out there.") Compelling visions are always a step or two beyond what today seems realistic.

What do you most fear in committing yourself to actively pursuing and achieving this vision? Is your vision meaningful enough for you, where you are willing to take a step or two forward, in spite of the fear?

What will you do now to take the next steps on your journey to the future?

Visions to Grow Your Organization

If your responses to the previous questions focused more on a personal future, we now invite you to spend some time thinking about the future destination you would like your organization to reach. Rather than repeating, take a minute to go back and re-look at the same questions that you have just spent time with. This time think about your answers relative to growing your organization, not just yourself.

In a nutshell, if your organization were to become everything you could imagine, what would you really want it to be? What would "moving across the street," or "building a space tourism company" look like in your work? If you became either the best of the best, or the only ones who do what you do, what would you most like that to be?

Don't be afraid to think in bold and daring ways. Most of us tend to think much too small, probably because it is more comfortable or because it raises the chances of success in our minds. But remember this. It is highly unlikely that when Howard Schultz joined Starbucks in 1982, or when Sam Walton opened the first Wal-Mart in Rogers AR, in 1962, that either of them could have ever imagined what their respective companies would have actually grown into by 2006. You just never know what is truly possible. Growth requires imagination, so start giving your organization the creative thinking time and effort it deserves.

Chapter 6: Building Commitment

Several years ago, Steve was talking with the manager of a group about his team. To understand the lay of the land, Steve asked the guy how many people he had working for him. His answer was a bit of a surprise. The manager responded, "about half!" He wasn't too far off, as a typical comment from any one of the direct reports about the work situation was something like, "I am working hard enough where I won't get fired, and making enough money that I don't want to quit." The remainder of the comment would tail off after that. It was easy to see that something was certainly missing in this group.

Over the years we have heard several managers lament about the lack of passion and vision in their organizations. There appears to be some validity in their observations. Research by authors Kanter and Mirvis in the early 1990's indicated that nearly half (47 percent) of workers in an American organization fell into the category called Cynics. One of the key descriptions of a cynic was an individual who had emotionally checked out of the job. Gallup followed up in the early 2000's by looking at the levels of worker engagement in organizations. Their findings showed that about 71 percent of people were either non-engaged (55 percent), or actively non-engaged (16 percent).

However you slice the research, it will be much harder to grow any organization if a large percentage of its people have little fire in their belly to take on that challenge. The people who are willing to risk stepping out and determining new ways of doing things have that fire—not just in their bellies, but in their hearts.

This leads us back to a fundamental question. Do you believe that you can do anything to generate more passion and vision within your people? Or are those traits something that a person simply does or does not have, regardless of the circumstances? The people featured throughout this book certainly had commitment to whatever it was they were pursuing. And like many examples of great leadership, they faced situations that could have, perhaps even should have, extinguished their fires.

We invite you to ponder, do you work for organizations with a recruiting strategy based on seeking out and hiring cynics or non-engaged people? Think about yourself when you were searching for a new job. When you heard that you had been hired, did you not feel some excitement? Were you not committed to work hard and be successful? Might you felt a sense of personal pride, in knowing that you must have been the best of many other candidates for the position? Do these things sound like the attributes of a cynic?

Organizations do not hire cynics or non-engaged people—they create them. Over time, life in an organization simply sucks the life out of a lot of people's passions and dreams, and they become less and less committed. Would you expect that these people are going to enthusiastically put forth much time and effort in conceiving new growth ideas, and then put themselves at risk to prove them?

We believe everyone is capable of having passion and dreams about something. We also believe that if emotional commitment (and engagement) can be sapped by disheartening experiences, it can also be built or strengthened by the right kinds of experiences. In fact, we see strengthening other people's commitment as one of the key responsibilities of leadership. We also see an emotionally committed workforce as a distinct advantage in a competitive environment.

A Special Commitment

Commitment becomes an impetus for growth in organizations when vision and passion are alive. The place just feels differently when leaders exercise their responsibility to share the vision and communicate passionately about the company and your association with it. It is senior leadership's role to inspire every employee, colleague, vendor and customer about the difference the company's products, services and culture can make for the world. The painting of the aspirational future and the subsequent passion for the business builds employee and customer commitment.

But, could commitment be raised to an even higher level—one that achieves employee and customer *devotion*? When devotion is present in your organization, the effort to achieve the vision is ratcheted up to a level not believed possible. And devotion moves people to work diligently so the company or business unit will grow and experience success. But, devotion doesn't happen without senior leadership leaving the spectator stands and actively engaging in the fray by sharing the vision and inspiring passion in the organization. Leadership earns devotion. It isn't freely given by employees and customers. And when leadership does work hard at vision and passion-building, devoted employees find innovative ways for the company and business unit to succeed. They view this as their responsibility.

We met Caroline Moore of Struever Bros. Eccles & Rouse in the late 90's. Bill Struever brought us to the company to work with his leadership team and to support the firm as it developed its vision and culture. From the first meeting with her, Caroline was an impressive professional. In her role as Director of Commercial Development, she was striving to establish SBER's niche as the premier mid-Atlantic adaptive re-use developer. Her striving often turned into struggling because she was still learning the business while trying to develop her leadership philosophy. Caroline was always focused on building great projects and developing people. She was unique because her conversations were about improving the process and enhancing her leadership. But, the most important influence on her growth was Bill Struever and his vision and passion. Caroline would be sitting in meetings or attending different events and she could hear Bill Struever whispering the vision in her ear. She would then remind the group that SBER is "focused on transforming the economy, confidence and spirit of our cities." Struever was not only the architect of the vision but he also promoted it to the staff and the firm's clients. Caroline respected Bill's knowledge and experience but her professional growth and loyalty to the firm was based on Struever's inspiring vision and passion for the business.

The SBER vision and passion drove her devotion to the firm. Today, Caroline Moore is the Chief Operating Officer of Real Estate Development for SBER. She is also the senior executive for the SBER brand, devoting her efforts and passion on transforming and sharpening every aspect of the company's business model. Since starting her employment with SBER in 1986, her career growth has been extraordinary and well-deserved. Her success has only been matched by the dynamic growth of the firm. Caroline's devotion and the high employee engagement at SBER originates from the firm's pioneering personality that honors its roots by transforming real estate into valuable commodities and by creating neighborhoods with economic and social value.

This devotion to "something" moves individuals to turn passion into real results. When vision and passion stirs the embers, the flames are ready to break out. SBER is a renowned and high growth development firm because it has completed the hard work—creating and sharing the vision and building passion with its employees and customers. Unique, difficult and rewarding projects will always be a part of the firm's future. And so will devoted employees and customers if senior leadership presents a clear, compelling vision and energizes the workforce through their passion.

You probably have a Bill Struever, Nancy Brogan, Alice Coles, or Burt Rutan working with you right now. You have people such as them, with comparable passion and vision about how to grow your business and create committed, even devoted associates such as Caroline Moore. Be truthful with yourself. Do you know who they are? Are you creating an environment where they can leverage their strengths for the good of the organization.

Leading Toward Commitment

The road to more effectively leading people toward commitment, even devotion often starts by examining our own beliefs and assumptions. So read through the following questions and ponder your answers. You need to be clear on where you stand before you can know where to start.

1) Do you believe that a number of your people have passion about the work they are responsible for doing? Or do you believe that people who have passion tend to work somewhere else?

2) If you were to honestly assess the level of passion that exists within your organization for your goals and purposes, where would the overall score fall on a scale of 1 (low) to 10 (high)? What evidence could you offer to support your answer? What is contributing to the score?

3) To what extent do you believe that having a compelling vision of the future is important, and not just somewhat of a leadership fad?

4) How often do you engage your people in vision discussions — about things you want to be doing and destinations you want to be reaching?

We have discovered a common theme about this topic of building commitment. Throughout our exploration into the issue of passion, we noticed that a large number of people said that what most stirred their fires of passion was in providing service to others. For some their passion might have been about better education systems for kids of all ages. (They are particularly inspired by Nancy Brogan's efforts!) For others it has been about community affairs — from providing shelter and clothing to those in need, to picking up trash. We have come across people inspired by their religious beliefs, and all aspects of helping others associated with their faith. And yes, we have even come across many who are deeply committed to their customers — serving them in the best ways possible.

If serving others in some capacity is so meaningful for so many people, don't you think it is possible for them to find some ways in their work to fulfill that need? Are there steps you can take to help them tap into that passion of service and help them live it more in their daily work?

In the workplace we have heard and seen much more passion displayed in terms of taking care of the customer, associates, and other colleagues, than we have in terms of fulfilling shareowner expectations. Too often a zero sum mindset has been reinforced, with the belief being that customers and fellow employees have to lose in order for shareowners to win. The conclusion we have drawn is that shareowner return is not a primary passion of people throughout organizations, at least outside of the senior ranks. Yes, they want shareowner value to increase, because many of them are shareowners of their own companies. They are just more passionate about the other things that result in shareowner value, things like devoted customers, great work environments, quality products, world class processes, and so forth.

Actions to take:

If you want to increase the level of commitment that people have to you and the work you do, here are a few things for you to consider. Remember, there is no "just add water and stir" formula for success. You must believe that you can positively influence other peoples' commitment, and you have to approach it in a way that is authentic for you.

* Talk to other people about their passions. Ask them questions about what gives them joy and fulfillment? Really understand what lights them up.
* Share things you are passionate about with them. Show by example that it is okay to feel devoted to something.
* Talk up your organization, what it does and the value it provides. Counterbalance the endless preoccupation on the numbers by helping them see the contributions that the company makes to the community or to the world. Show them how the organization affords many of its members the opportunity to serve on boards, do volunteer work, and coach little league. These things, along with foundations, endowments and other financial gifts, make an impact and give people a sense of pride about the place they work.
* Talk to people about their dreams. Find out what mark they want to leave in the world, what they want to be known or remembered for.

- Involve people in helping create a future vision for your group or organization. Ask them for their thoughts.
- Publicly recognize people for their spirited energy when they are demonstrating passion, and for their responsible stewardship to the long term success of the business when they put forth visionary ideas.
- Help people feel indispensable to your organization's success by challenging them with tough, but meaningful opportunities, and letting them know how much you genuinely need them.
- Bring in a role model of passion or vision to talk with your people. Let them get to "feel" the energy associated with passion and vision.
- Ask people to describe how their work needs to be different in order for them to feel more excited about it.
- Include discussions about passion and vision as part of regular meetings. Our guess is you spend more than enough time reviewing past actions and results. Spend time on helping people become more energized about shaping the future.
- Deal with the persistent cynics. Hear them out, understand them, challenge them to step up and encourage them to add value. You have many options from which to choose in dealing with cynics. You just cannot ignore or endlessly tolerate them.

COMPETENCE

Passion and vision provide the much needed fuel to people who are willing to take on the status quo and initiate new and better ways of doing things. For those of you who have stepped up to this challenge, you know how draining it can be. It seems like there is always another obstacle to overcome, whether it is something or someone. If you lose your emotional commitment, it will be much easier for those outside forces to overcome your efforts. You will then have to tolerate a lot more change being done to you.

As powerful as commitment is, it was not enough by itself to guarantee success for the role models we observed who challenged the process. They also possessed a great deal of competence, and the attributes of expertise and experience were vital in helping them make their lasting marks.

Consider all the knowledge that Burt Rutan and his associates had to have in order to design and build a vehicle that could go into space and return safely with the pilot and aircraft in tact. Or perhaps you have come across Jim Cramer, the "high octane" host of television and radio programs on investing. His uncanny ability to answer almost any question from any caller about any stock comes from the detailed knowledge of some 2000 companies and their respective industries, lodged in his head. Let's just say Burt, Jim and people like them know what they are talking about.

Experience is another key part of competence. Might it had been more difficult for Gail Mayville to come up with a solution for Ben & Jerry's waste problem, if she had not grown up on a farm and had experience with recycling? And wouldn't you expect that Laird Hamilton's life on a surfboard would make him much more likely to harness a 70-foot wave than a novice surfer who was still challenged by a ten footer?

Think about this. In your mind, what is the most prevalent reason for sports teams at the college or professional level to bring in a new coach? It is usually because the administrators or owners are seeking change. Given the enormous competitive pressures to win, they easily become dissatisfied with their team's current levels of success. They realize they must fundamentally change a lot of key things if they have any hope of becoming a winner. And they will pay big bucks for a coach who has the talent or capability to lead that change and take the team to glory. The coaches, who are most highly sought after, have proven they can produce results. They have incredible knowledge and vast experiences, from which they have developed the set of skills needed to take their teams to a new level of success. Competence is a clear differentiator between a great coach who can create a new system for winning and a mediocre coach who cannot.

The same is true in other areas of business and life. Competence, one's level of expertise and collective set of experiences, is a key that can unlock the door to great breakthroughs. In the next chapters we will explore more deeply the powerful concepts of expertise and experience, the attributes that define Competence.

Chapter 7: A Head Full of Know-How: Expertise

In 1980 the daughter of Candy Lightner was struck by a car that was driven by a drunk driver. From that moment on, Candy began a non-stop effort to change the laws of the land, so that no other parents would ever have to experience the devastating loss of a child at the hands of a drunk. As you may know Candy went on to become the founder of Mothers Against Drunk Drivers (MADD). Today, the drinking and driving laws, and perhaps more significantly the social acceptance of drinking and driving, have dramatically changed.

Can you imagine what her challenge must have been like? When one of the authors lived in Texas during the early 1980's, it was legal and quite acceptable to be "sucking down a cold one" as you drove. Driving with a beer after work was almost as common as driving with a cup of coffee on the way to work. It was not at all an exaggeration to say that some believed they had a "God-given right" to have a beer while driving.

This was just part of the adversity that Candy Lightner had to take on.

In the 70's and 80's many people drove after having a few, even too many drinks. No one really thought too much about the implications, as it was a common occurrence. Is it possible that the prevailing attitude might have been something like, "it is a shame about Candy and others like her, but drinking and driving just isn't that big of an issue across the country?"

It is impossible to tell how prevalent this attitude may have been, but whatever did exist just added more adversity for Candy Lightner to overcome.

There was no doubt that Candy had great passion about her cause and a clear vision of what she wanted to accomplish. But for her, this extraordinary commitment was not enough. Success required much more than desire, anger, or a broken heart. She not only had to figure out how to create an organization of devoted supporters, but she and the rest of her colleagues also had to understand how to write, sponsor, and promote new laws. She had to become knowledgeable about both the written and unwritten rules of the legislative game.

MADD is now in its third decade of changing lives, public opinion, and public policy. People everywhere believe that the organization is fulfilling its mission to stop drunk driving, support victims of this violent crime, and prevent underage drinking. And due to its success as a charitable non-profit, the organization itself has become a recognized expert in helping other grass root organizations, with little more than strong passion and a great dream, become a real force for change.

Expertise is vital to move the status quo in a new direction. You must have a substantial level of education or knowledge about the things you are trying to change. Although breakthrough ideas can come from people, with little or no knowledge of the subject being challenged, it is hard to imagine that people lacking a comparable level of Burt Rutan's knowledge could have ever pulled off SpaceShipOne. We also suspect that Carly Fiorina, even as a CEO, had to do an enormous amount of knowledge-building homework before determining whether HP's acquisition of Compac was even worth pursuing.

By the way, we have to chuckle every time we come across young adults about to graduate college who shout with glee, "Finally, no more homework!" Are they ever in for a big surprise, at least if they ever intend to lead an effort to change something of importance. Continuous homework is part of the price to pay for expertise—and growth.

Value of Learning

Remember Alice Coles, who led her neighbors from the complete squalor of one side of the street in Bayview, VA to a brand new life on the other? She clearly demonstrated the importance of gaining knowledge and expertise in achieving big aspirations. She realized that building a new community was going to take a huge sum of money, which they simply did not have. To acquire it, she and others were going to have to become much smarter in many different areas—such as fundraising, politics, lobbying, organizational skills and so forth. Alice later remarked how people took her under their wings and taught her and others the basics they most needed to know to convince the government and other private foundations to finance their dream.

Could these people now be considered experts in each of these areas? We assume not. But they did continue to develop their expertise in order to keep plowing ahead. Even more importantly, they never hesitated to rely on others outside of the community who had even greater levels of expertise in these areas. And since those outside experts were in short supply, the now more intelligent Bayview leaders were able to use them more effectively to get more money and more results more quickly.

Leaders are said to be life long learners. Their work is about shaping the future to make it better than today. Because it is the future, there are no guaranteed answers about what will work best and what will not. Those answers have to be discovered by questioning and challenging the methods and norms as they exist today. This is why people who lead growth are frequently involved in tests, trials, pilots, experiments, and so forth. Yet it is crucial to remember that breakthrough discoveries are not made simply from the test and trials themselves, but from the education and knowledge—the learning—gained from them.

One of the characteristics we have discovered about people who have successfully pushed through the status quo and led growth, is that they have enormous credibility in their area of expertise. People agree that these champions of change know a great deal about their specialty, even if their goals seem wrong or misguided.

Given the thousands of BMW fans that responded to the "Stop Chris Bangle" petition on the internet, one could assume that the dramatic change he was instigating in the physical appearance of the various BMW models was not universally accepted. At the same time, there was no question that Chris Bangle had credibility in car design. Otherwise he would have never been offered the prestigious position of Chief Designer, nor won the acclaim of the design community.

Expertise is one of the key attributes that determines credibility. For a person to be believable in a field of endeavor, he or she is expected to have significant knowledge and wisdom about it. It seems quite obvious doesn't it? Can there even be such a person as a non-credible expert?

Entertaining Expertise

In 2000, a new television program hit the airwaves that featured characters who each had enormous levels of education and knowledge, especially in the sciences. It was called *CSI* (*Crime Scene Investigation*), and it soon became one of the most frequently watched programs every week. The basic premise of this "who done it" was the discovery of a lifeless body and the CSI team being called into action to figure out what happened. What viewers learned very quickly was how much expertise the CSI's had, as they went about solving the crimes. Whether it was in-depth knowledge of physics, biology, ballistics, or even insects, this group used the unbending principles and laws of science to come up with unconventional, yet valid solutions for what appeared to be unsolvable cases. This was one of those shows where viewers could actually learn something if they paid attention. And it became so popular that it spawned two sister *CSI* programs, which were both successful as well.

Although only a TV show, it reinforced for us that expertise, the deep knowledge and intelligence that comes from sources like formal education, curiosity, tinkering and so forth, is required in order to figure out how to solve problems that do not appear to be solvable. You've already read about a few, such as how to get onto a 70-foot wave, get parents more directly involved in their children's education, or provide clean water around the world. Expertise is also needed for challenges more close to home, like increasing sales in a declining market or figuring out how to recruit top producers who are committed to staying with you.

Before we leave the example from television, consider this for a moment. Given the kind of programs that seem most likely to be hits, would you as a TV executive have been willing to risk a sizable amount of money, as well as your own reputation, on a program dealing with experts in science? At the time, that in itself might have seemed like a huge gamble.

Profitably growing the business in a dog eat dog industry like television sometimes requires people to challenge traditional thinking and take the risk of trying something new. The same is true for you in your industry.

The Expertise Factor in Business

How many times have you read a press release from a company when it missed its earnings target? Most read the same, something like: "the shortfall is blamed on higher (or lower) than expected interest rates, fluctuations in currency markets, political economic policies, a shortfall in industry demand, or increased cost of supplies." The specific reasons might vary slightly, but these announcements are quite consistent in citing factors external to the company. Just once we would like to read one that said,

> *"Our earnings were off because we have not been smart enough to recognize and act upon the subtle and not so subtle changes taking place in our industry. We have not kept up with technology and have missed several obvious clues that clearly pointed to changing customer preferences and shifting economics in supply chain management. We have realized that we do not have enough valuable know-how in our various lines of business to break away from our old, established ways of doing things and successfully compete against some very clever, future oriented competitors.*

Funny how you never read that response in a press release. But the lack of expertise to successfully compete in today's ever-changing marketplace is the exact conversation that frequently takes place within struggling companies, by people who really care and are courageous enough to talk truthfully. Many organizations today simply lack the levels of expertise they need to consistently deliver solid results, in a world where the playing field changes literally every day. And given the eye-popping salaries that are tossed around for perceived experts, organizations seem certainly willing to pay for it.

Broad expertise is critical for the person at the top of the corporation. When Carly Fiorina was forced out of the top position at HP in February 2005, it was reported that the board of directors was disappointed by her inability to transform the plodding technology giant into a more nimble innovator. She had failed to slash costs and boost revenues as quickly as the directors had hoped. By the way, how many CEO's has that been said about? You might recall that Fiorina had overcome fierce opposition by board director and family member Walter Hewlett, when the company followed Fiorina's lead to acquire Compac.

It is interesting to note that a comment about her ousting from one of the board members was that her firing in no way reflected a change in direction of the general road map. The board just thought a new set of capabilities in the CEO was called for. One could conclude the board did not think she possessed the competence or leadership skills to lead the company forward. Keep in mind that the skills needed for determining a strategic direction can be different from those needed for executing it.

It looks as if press releases about struggling companies are now beginning to point the finger more directly at CEO expertise (or lack thereof). We just find that disappointing results are seldom caused solely by the CEO. Bringing in a new top person with different capabilities is not necessarily wrong. It just may not be enough, especially if the collective level of expertise throughout the organization does not change.

Opening New Doors

Expertise can be a tremendous asset when attempting to change the competitive landscape and create new growth markets. Think about this. A few years ago, how wise would it have been to invest additional money into yet another portable stereo device? Almost every company involved in some way or the other with electronics was producing their own version of a CD player. Although these devices were inexpensive to produce, they were not generating high margins for the brand owner. And we suspect that even the top brands were unable to earn a premium margin. With a number of viable alternatives to choose from, each having virtually identical features, why pay more for one over another? Portable music CD players had clearly become a commodity.

But another band of innovators, possessing different expertise saw gold in that arena, and along came the iPod®. Apple likely had the capability to buy (or maybe even make) a CD assembly with all kinds of neat features, and put a snazzy casing around it. But instead, they capitalized on a different set of capabilities, technical as well as marketing, and dramatically changed the mature market of portable CD's into a fresh and very lucrative new growth opportunity.

It is very exciting to see how individuals or companies parlay their expertise into changing the rules of the game and pursue groundbreaking growth.

Stop and think once again about your own personal role models of people who have accomplished something that required them to challenge and reshape current and accepted ways of thinking. Would you say they had some level of expertise, or was blind luck and persistence their keys to success?

Taking Stock

For all of you non-accountants, how would you feel if you were challenged to come up with a new set of progressive, yet legal accounting processes for your organization to adopt? You would be under a severe time crunch and your pay would be directly impacted by your results. Given the choice, would you volunteer or politely decline.

Our point is that many times an organization's people are expected to challenge the process and immediately produce improved results in areas they have little experience with or knowledge about. And their managers wonder why these people don't sustain a high degree ‹ enthusiasm about the challenge or immediately produce great results.

Gaining expertise in an area is an arduous task. It requires that a person have some degree of interest in or compelling reason to put forth the effort to keep learning. It is the relationship between passion and competence. When people have passion—like eliminating drunk drivers—it helps them want to continue struggling to acquire the knowledge they need to succeed.

There is another factor that makes gaining expertise so difficult of a pursuit. It is that ever so seductive part of an individual's make-up known as ego or arrogance. It is easy to believe that because I might currently be recognized as having great expertise in a subject, I will always be an expert. I have passed my final exams with flying colors in this subject, and don't need to study any longer.

It is disheartening to come across people who believe that the high degree of knowledge they possess today entitles them to remain a recognized expert in the new and very different world of tomorrow. Think about one example—today's world of advanced vision correction surgery. We can't imagine many experts in yesterday's procedure of radial keratonomy (RK) are growing their businesses, if they are all thumbs with today's much better and safer laser-based procedures.

By now, you have probably been thinking about what you have passion for in your career and personal life. Maybe you have even thought through a vision related to your passion, some kind of end you would really like to achieve. Now it is time for you to examine whether or not you have the expertise to get you to that destination.

Take a few minutes to read over and reflect on the following questions. They serve an important purpose. They will help you determine what you personally need to learn in order to ride your personal 70-foot wave, and how your organization may need to change to elevate its collective expertise. Be prepared—this will take some work.

our Expertise:

1. In what areas do you wish you were or feel you need to be smarter? (Don't respond with the answers you think a boss or a spouse might give for you. Answer honestly for yourself.)

2. Why do you feel the need to grow in these particular areas? For example, are you having trouble keeping up because of the pace of change? Or, are you involved in something new or different for you?

3. What do you think it will take for you to increase your knowledge about one or more of the items you listed above? (Think about various methods such as formal class work, a dedicated coach or teacher, hands-on experience, or others.) How do you learn the best?

4. What can you do to increase your organization's commitment to raising the levels of expertise in all parts?

5. In what ways are you being forced to compensate for a lack of expertise? Have you avoided working with new people? Would other say you are continuing to do things pretty much the same way you have always done them? Does it seem like you spend more time justifying or defending your actions than you use to?

6. Reflecting back on one thing about which you know you need to become more knowledgeable, what is an achievable goal that you can set that will help you start making immediate progress? Write it down, take a deep breath and start putting it into play, right now.

Your Organization's Expertise:

1. What are the top competencies that your organization possesses? To what extent will these ensure success going forward?

2. In what does your organization need to become more expert? Why did you answer the way you did? What is your evidence?

3. To what extent does your organization invest in the ongoing development of talent?

4. What can you do to increase your organization's commitment to raising the levels of expertise in all parts?

Chapter 8: Been There, Done That and Learned from It: Experience

It is impossible to be considered competent without experience. And it is extremely difficult to break through accepted ways of doing things and initiate change or growth with little or no real world, hands-on application.

Some of you may be familiar with the story, *The Right Stuff*, about the fearless test pilots who risked life and limb to pave America's way into space. There were many different definitions of the term, but having the right stuff certainly referred to attributes like guts, persistence, heart and so forth. One of the featured characters was a man named Chuck Yeager, who became the first person to ever fly a plane faster than the speed of sound. Although commonplace today, it was considered an unbelievable accomplishment when it occurred in 1947. In the autobiographical book about his life, Chuck Yeager commented about having the Right Stuff. He said:

"The question annoys me because it implies that a guy who has the right stuff was born that way. I was born with unusually good eyesight and coordination. I was mechanically oriented. My nature was to stay cool in tight spots. Is that the right stuff? All I know is that I worked my tail off to learn how to fly and worked hard at it all the way. And in the end, the one big reason why I was better than average as a pilot was because I flew more than anybody else. If there is such a thing as the right stuff in piloting, then it is experience."

Time in the cockpit, is the key to breakthroughs in almost any aspect of life.

Breakthroughs in standard surgical procedures come from the surgeons, who have actually performed them on countless occasions, not from analysts working for HO who have never been in an operating room. Ideas for re-engineering of a sophisticated inventory management process come from the people who have experiences with the rocess everyday. They know and understand both the obvious and the subtle things that will happen when change is introduced. And they know how various points all along the process will be impacted.

Some people hold the point of view that a lack of experience might be more advantageous when attempting to create a novel way of doing something. With no practical experience, a person would not be jaundiced in his or her thinking and could look at something in a completely fresh and new way. What do you think about that? Agree or disagree?

It is not unheard of to read about a newly appointed CEO who came into a business with little or no experience in the particular industry, and then commenced to shake up and change virtually everything in leading the company to prosperity. Lou Gerstner who led the turnaround of IBM during the 1990's would seemingly fit that mold. And when you think about it, no U.S. president, upon taking office the very first day, ever had the hands-on experience of leading an entire country on an international stage.

Although the business executives may have lacked experience with the companies or industries they took on, the thing to remember is they certainly had deep experience in the key aspects of operating a successful business, and what it took to turn around a struggling company. Similar things can be said about presidents. They have likely had wide experiences in coalition building, developing and passing legislation, foreign diplomacy and many other competencies crucial to the job. They are by no means novices to the responsibilities awaiting them.

Many growth breakthroughs are clearly the result of a team effort. In these situations, collective experience resides within the team instead of merely within one person. That means for the team to succeed, each person must have the kind of experiences that allows him or her to be the best—for their role on the team. On an Indy team, it is the engineers and mechanics, whose lives are spent on top of, underneath and inside of engines, who are constantly figuring out how to squeeze out that extra bit of horsepower that could be the difference between winning and the middle of the pack. And it is the miles of blinding straight-aways and thousands of "left hand turns" at 200 mph that gives a driver the sixth sense to know if the tires are a bit too soft or the wings need an ever so slight adjustment.

Remember Nancy Brogan, the principal from Ditmas? Did she need to have deep experience in explaining how the Windows® operating system worked to the parents of her students receiving computers? Did Alice Coles, whose vision created a new life for her neighbors in Bayview VA need to have experience in understanding the nuances of applying for a government grant? The answer in both cases is no. But whoever was in the respective cockpits of computer training or grant application certainly did.

What Does Experience Mean

In organization's today, an exchange about *experience* offers up an interesting discussion. You're no doubt familiar with the philosophical question: does a person working in a given field for half a decade have five years of experience, or one year of experience repeated five times over? Given the rate of change in the world today, that question does deserve some attention.

Experience is about dealing with new and different situations, not just repetition of the same thing over and over again. Think about the shade tree mechanic, who had worked on cars for a quarter of a century. He was so experienced with various kinds of engines, he could tell just by listening if a motor was running rich or lean. And no matter what kind of carburetor, he knew how to adjust it to make the air/fuel mix just right, so the car would run better and get better mileage.

During the mid-1970s, the shade tree mechanic would have been in demand as a next door neighbor. He would keep all the cars on the cul-de-sac finely tuned without incurring the cost of taking it into the shop. But then something happened. Engine technology changed and carburetors ceased to exist. The right mixture of air and fuel, like almost everything else on a car, became computer controlled. And almost every year, fuel injection systems, emission control systems and all that other magical stuff hidden under the hood designed to keep the engine running properly, have continued to be improved.

So here is a pertinent question. Of what use is the shade tree mechanic's 25 years of experience today, if no one drives a car with a carburetor? Doesn't he now need to have solid experiences with today's engines, if he expects to continue to add value to car owners and compete with other mechanics?

Consider the situation of the mechanic in today's context of constant change and challenge. Because he had years and years of experiences working around engines in general, do you think it will be easier or harder for him to gain the expertise and experiences needed to be successful with the contemporary engine? Will any part of those past twenty five years be helpful?

Our definitive answer to that question is "who knows!" He may have a general comfort around any kind of engine, and be wide open to learning more and more about new ones. There are also certain principles of an internal combustion engine that would likely continue to be very applicable even with today's advanced technology. So at least some of his experiences would still serve him well. (That is, until a team of challengers finally overcome the current obstacles of the electric or solar engine, and create the breakthrough which renders the gasoline engine obsolete. Then, perhaps, even less of his quarter century of hands-on investment would be useful.)

On the other hand, he could be so stuck in his ways that in his mind the old carburetion system is still the only "right way" for an engine to operate, and he will never be able to accept the current reality. Hopefully, there will be enough people in his neighborhood with old clunkers that he can continue to use his expertise from experience to some advantage. "Stuck in the past" was clearly not a characteristic found in people that initiated change and generated new growth opportunities. We doubt if you are surprised at that!

People who step up to challenge current ways of operating to raise the standards of performance or achievement must ensure they are continuing to have *useful and relevant experiences*. The SpaceShipOne team worked with, computer modeled, tested, and experimented with different materials than were used on the plane that Chuck Yeager first flew beyond the sound barrier. Whatever experiences they had with the old materials were not enough to achieve their goal. Only Laird Hamilton could tell you accurately how many different kinds of surfboards he has ridden or how many falls he had to experience to finally figure out the exact approach for standing up on and riding a 70-foot wave. On the other side, Alice Coles, the architect of the new Bayview VA, was smart enough to realize that she did not have the expertise or experience needed to put all the pieces together to implement a new community. So she went out and found someone who did, and that person's project management experience was a key ingredient in their collective success.

The Value of Experience

One of the very most important purposes that experience serves for those who are up to challenging for change is this. It provides a person with *immediate options when unexpected things begin to happen*, opposed to leaving him or her paralyzed. And when one is attempting something new for the first time, the unexpected will always happen.

During one flight while piloting an X1-A aircraft at nearly 1,650 mph (over twice the speed of sound), Chuck Yeager found himself in an uncontrollable spin, plummeting toward certain death. He was being violently knocked around the cockpit, and the face plate of his helmet became fogged, rendering him blind. As coolly as he could, he started thinking about and quickly trying a lot of different remedies to stop the spiral. After falling 51,000 feet in 51 seconds, he finally found the right combination, regained control, and was able to survive. (And most of us think a 100-foot drop on a roller coaster is death-defying!)

Yeager, himself, attributed his survival to instinct and pure luck.

However, when you read his account of that flight, Yeager made a very telling comment that indicates there was something else happening besides luck. During his heart-stopping plunge, he had taken a variety of actions that finally left the plane in a "normal spin" at the 30,000-foot level. At that moment Yeager realized *he knew how to get out of that spin*, because as he said, "I had spun every airplane imaginable." About 5,000 feet later he popped out of the spin and shortly thereafter, landed safely.

It is a pretty safe bet that an explosive crash would have been the result for anyone with less experience. Fortunately for Yeager, his depth of experience allowed him to respond with the solutions that ultimately saved his life. Experience (breadth and depth) is the driver for successful growth.

Just so you will know, there will always be occurrences of falling or spinning out of control when you are trying to breakthrough barriers and achieve something great. It is an unavoidable part of the territory. The question is, do you have enough experience to pop out and regain the upper hand when the spin-outs occur?

At the large public accounting and consulting firms (e.g. Deloitte, Ernst & Young, etc.), the most important position is the senior accountant, senior tax or senior consultant role. It is the position responsible for executing the client engagement plan, managing the budget, directing and evaluating the young staff, developing on-site relationships with the client, and preparing the engagement report. This "senior" role is critical to delivering the engagement on budget with strong technical reporting and solid client relationships. This difficult and challenging situation is reserved for professionals with a minimum of three years experience and extensive firm education. This is the profile. But, with high turnover at the senior level, these assignments are being filled through "battlefield promotions" by professionals with one to two years experience. They are not technically or emotionally prepared for this work. They have not walked in the footsteps of a senior enough times to be effective. We define it as "lacking length in experience."

For client service firms, this scenario happens far too often. Difficult client service situations are being offered to top notch, but inexperienced professionals. They are not prepared to deal with technical issues, to handle young, hard-charging staff, to cozy up with clients and to answer all the partners' inquiries. This inexperience is a major reason why client service companies forfeit growth. The lack of experienced people means being unable to deliver the level of service for business retention and growth. Business expansion goes on the back burner without the availability of competent, experienced people to pass on the value proposition and the brand promise to the customer.

This scenario is also a dilemma for the less experienced professionals themselves. They want the opportunity to demonstrate their talents in an important situation, but most "junior people" realize that their inexperience limits the engagement playbook. They also know that this limitation can create a disgruntled client, because now the client must provide additional training and staff support in order to achieve the results agreed to in the contract. So how will the "lite senior" respond, knowing that the outcome will impact his or her professional growth and position for promotion, the continued relationship with the client, and the development of the other staff involved?

Ultimately, firm and professional growth depends on experience. Experience—great when you have it; tough when you don't.

Can you envision a team of seasoned ER doctors mobilizing to treat a victim of a horrible accident? In order to save the person's life, they have to act immediately. There may be no time or means to retrieve a history, so they cannot precisely know how the patient will respond to their life-saving actions. Because of the patient's condition, some actions taken by the doctors might be considered non-traditional, even radical. But should the patient's blood pressure suddenly drop, an artery burst, or heart beat unexpectedly stop, they do not freeze with shock, like a first year medical student might. Just the opposite occurs. They immediately reach into their deep repertoire of experiences and without delay, begin taking other steps in order to save the person's life.

Experience matters! It is important in every critical opportunity—

whether it is a professional medical team saving a life, a wealth management expert counseling an executive on retirement options, or an M&A consultant advising a Board of Directors on a potential acquisition. Experience makes the difference.

When attempting something new for the first time, you can never know for certain what exactly will happen. Will riding a 70-foot wave be entirely different than one 30-feet high? Will pigs actually eat Ben & Jerry's ice cream waste? Will people buy a stylish looking BMW or take an OTC medicine for 14 straight days?

Let us offer one last example of why experience is so necessary for those who are committed to challenging and growing. Remember what it was like when you first learned to drive a car with a stick shift and a clutch. If you are like most, starting the car in first gear was the real challenge. Did you stall the motor a few times? Did you also burn a little tread off the tires? Do you remember feeling like a bull rider, because of the way the car would buck and bounce?

But with enough practice, you finally figured it out. You learned the right motion for letting out the clutch, and the precise moment to start applying the gas. And all was right with the world—until you had to stop for a red light or stop sign at the crest of a hill. And no matter where you were or the time of day, there always seemed to be another car right behind you, seemingly inches from your back bumper. Do you remember that—how panicky you felt because you just knew you were going to roll backwards? Remember how you also worried that you would probably stall the engine as you tried to recover, and then the driver behind you would start blasting his horn, and pretty soon people all around you would start pointing at you and laughing at your bumbling incompetence. Do you remember that?

Here's the lesson to take from your somewhat painful and embarrassing memories about driving a stick. If you are going to challenge the accepted ways things are done, there will be hills and some of them will be pretty steep. If your experiences are limited to driving strictly on level ground or downhill, (the status quo), you will never make it very far from where you started. Proficiency at shifting in these situations is necessary, but clearly not enough to conquer the hills. You will need to have the unsettling experiences of rolling backward a few times, stalling the car and feeling inadequate. You will have to learn how to apply the handbrake, how quickly to shift your foot to the gas, and so forth. You will literally need to know the feel of it and feel comes from experience. Isn't it interesting that the principles of shifting on a hill are no different than on level ground. But, you must vary your approach for these different situations or the results will be unsatisfactory. And it is experience that enables you to eventually learn the best approach.

Tinkering

People who challenge the way things are done and create new standards of performance and growth tend to have current and valuable experiences in the areas they are tackling. A technique or method used to gain that experience is through tinkering. That is a word we don't hear very frequently in most organizations.

Tinkering means adjusting or working with something in an experimental manner. Have you ever tinkered to learn more about something?

Tinkering can take on many forms. It could mean clicking on new menu items or strange looking icons on your computer to see what pops up. (Thank goodness for the undo key!) Attempting to fix a broken appliance, to see if it will work again is another example. So is adding your own flair to a recipe, like spicing up your cole slaw by sprinkling a little cilantro on it. You probably have tinkered in your life more than you realize.

But how is your work related tinkering going? Are you noodling around in an experimental way?

Trouble is, in the workplace people usually don't get paid for experimental work. So if a problem exists, the answer is to call in the outside experts to complete an exhaustive study, and then hope that over time a proposed solution will be developed and offered. You know the rest of the story. The proposal goes back and forth and if the stars actually do align, a decision for action is finally reached. Then you cross your fingers and hope the solution works as well in reality as it did on paper.

We are exaggerating to some degree and also concede that sometimes this is the only way to resolve an issue, especially ones that have substantial impact on your survival. But this is usually not the only approach for many of the challenges that occur. It is too costly and time consuming to bring in an expert for every opportunity. Sometimes you have to start messing with the problem yourself.

For example, you have to play with different agenda's if you are trying to make meetings more productive. You have to try asking different kinds of questions or looking for different experiences, if the new people you are hiring are not sticking around. You have to put different kinds of people together if you are trying to stimulate new ways of thinking. Leaders can initiate growth ideas in the organization without bringing in outside experts. Chris Bangle of BMW remarked that when he was growing up, he came from a family that used to build stuff. They were always tinkering with something. Those experiences continue to serve him well today.

Laird Hamilton did a lot of tinkering. One of the outcomes of his experimentation was the foil board, a kind of surfboard with a rudder suspended a couple of feet below it. With this design, the suspended rudder actually holds the board a foot or so above the top of the waves, so the rider is literally surfing on air. You have to see it to believe it!

Think about how much tinkering Olympic skiers have done with bindings, length and design of skis, types of poles, goggles, you name it. For them an experimental adjustment can mean the difference between the gold medal and oblivion.

In a typical year, Capital One, the large credit card and financial services company, would conduct over 80,000 tests in order to thoroughly focus and refine its marketing efforts. Their marketing professionals tested everything from advertising copy to price points to credit lines in order to ensure that they were matching customer priorities and preferences. We would call that a lot of tinkering.

In their direct marketing pieces they have tested different colors of paper, font styles, whether or not to include a telephone number, and so on. They viewed this tinkering as a direct means of increasing profitability. Could those kinds of tests really have much impact on the bottom line?

Think about their business. As a company they received millions of calls a month. By shortening those calls by a few seconds or even eliminating some of them through more finely tuned mail pieces, Capital One reaped huge cost savings. On the growth side, one campaign they conducted enabled the company to determine that it was sensible to increase customer credit lines and offer an extremely low fixed rate on a new card. During a three-month period, this tinkering brought $3 billion of incremental revenue from just one offer in one quarter.

Results like these, millions in cost savings and billions in additional revenue, happen when companies have experienced people involved in tinkering.

Beliefs and Experience

There is one other reason why experience is such a vital attribute for people who challenge norms and initiate ground breaking change for growth. It is hard for people to pursue something new and better if they do not believe it is even possible. Therefore, they will often times have to accept new beliefs. That is one of the reasons that vision is so important. It helps people see more clearly the potential likelihood of a new reality that today does not exist. But sometimes a vision, no matter how compelling it may seem, is not enough. It usually takes some kind of experience for people to allow beliefs to change, especially some of the truly deep-seated ones.

Perhaps you subscribe to the adage that "seeing is believing." With the exception of a magician causing the Empire State Building to disappear, it is easier and more comfortable to believe what you see. Think about the number of people who completely dismissed the notion that the Berlin Wall could ever come down, until they actually saw footage of thousands of people hammering it down, bit by bit. Or consider the number of non-believers who refuse to accept that a dramatically different new product line can ever be successful, until the numbers clearly prove it. (Was this viewpoint not held about the early iPod® by some analysts?) Seems there are a lot of people from Missouri, the "Show Me" state, who have to see it, before they can believe it.

Trailblazers who live in the growth frontier rarely have the definite proof up front. They must have faith in themselves and already believe in their growth opportunity before it is a sure thing. Like Greg Allgood with pursuing safe drinking water or Nancy Brogan by providing computers, they often times have to convince others to believe differently as well.

The reason the focus on beliefs is so important is this. For people to think or act in different ways they must first believe in different ways. Behavior change occurs after belief change. And it is experience that most directly drives those changes in beliefs.

We come across people all the time who are convinced that they cannot do something. That something might be learning a different language, becoming a better coach (or spouse), or speaking in public. But their original thinking soon begins to change. As they work at it and get some hands-on practice, they become better. And as they improve they become more comfortable, and pretty soon, they are performing at a good or even great level. We smile when we hear them say "I never believed I could ever do this," or something similar.

With experience they now believe they can do it. And even more importantly, they also start believing they can now conquer other challenges they would have originally viewed as impossible. Experience creates new awareness, raises confidence and impacts beliefs. We have met a lot of parents whose beliefs about their abilities to raise a child are much different for their second child, after the experience of learning from their first!

Reflect for a moment on these examples about experiences and beliefs.

- Did the experience of 9/11 shake any of your beliefs about your personal security, or that of our country or the world in general? Has it made you view the world differently?
- With the experience of the Berlin Wall coming down, do you think people are now more open to believing that freedom can occur in countries where it is still stifled today?
- How long would it take your belief about a respectful work environment to change if you were publicly humiliated for putting forth a novel, yet controversial idea to your boss?

The more significant the experience, the more quickly and deeply it can alter beliefs. We believe that if you think back on your life, you will be able to recall other experiences you have encountered that have influenced your beliefs.

For people to become more engaged in conceiving and advancing inventive ideas for stimulating growth, they must believe their efforts will be worthwhile and that they are capable of doing it. They must in actuality, believe before they see. Experience gives people the foundation to believe in those yet unproven opportunities, and to be better able to convince others, whose help they need, to join them.

Building Your Experience Base

Sometimes the only way to grow over the long haul is to learn by doing. It is impossible to computer model everything. Learning by doing usually implies some level of discomfort. You have to get out of the Comfort Zone in order to grow. That means you have to mentally (and sometimes physically) prepare yourself for mistakes, blunders, spins, and falls. Those are all part of learning. We have yet to meet a Black Diamond skier who has not fallen, on multiple occasions, on the Greens and the Blues. And we would bet a handsome sum that the pilot who flew Burt Rutan's SpaceshipOne into the record books was not making his initial solo flight that day.

People who defy the current ways of doing things and produce new ways to grow have mindsets that place high value on experiencing new things—and learning from them. How they come across to others, especially when they are in the Learning Zone, is of much less importance than what they are learning. Candy Lightner, Alice Coles, and every other person we have written about no doubt looked foolish at some time in their quests, simply because of lack of experience to accomplish what they had set out to change. But they plowed forward, got their hands and knees dirty, gained the experience, and ultimately produced some remarkable results

As you prepare to take on the challenge of further developing your level of experience, we want to pose some important questions for you to consider. You should be able to provide evidence to support your answer for each.

1. Are you willing to put yourself in new and potentially uncomfortable situations in order to learn?

2. Are you willing to attempt the more difficult slope and risk falling a few times? Will you deliberately move out of your comfort zone?

3. Can you clearly see a difference between making a mistake while learning and making a mistake due to lack of attention or some other reason?

4. Are you willing to look bad or foolish for some period of time?

5. How important is learning or doing something new to you? What if it means letting go of something that you are very competent in and admired for?

There are correct answers to each of these questions. Those are the ones that are the truth for you. No matter what you say in response to these questions, what you believe deep within, will ultimately guide your willingness to enhance your experiences. Just do not lose sight of the shade tree mechanic.

Before leaving this topic, give some thought to the following questions about your organization's current approach to experience. Your reflections will help determine whether your company has the experience to sustain its growth and prosperity, and overcome the status quo.

1. To what extent are people challenged with new opportunities to grow and apply new talents vs. doing the same work over and over?
2. What are some of the greatest lessons learned in your organization over the past few years? How would you rate your effectiveness in sharing those learnings across the organization?
3. In which areas do people need higher levels of experience so the organization can succeed in the future?

Remember, there is only one thing worse than learning from experience, and that is *not* learning from experience. In today's growth companies, people at every level understand that their current experience will not be enough to assure success in a world where everything continues to change around them.

Chapter 9: Building Competence

Have you ever read or heard about someone who has accomplished a great feat and then wondered how much of what this person did was attributed to inborn factors? That question is raised all the time about leaders—are they really born or made. Well there is some good news about competence. It is one of those things that people can learn and further develop. And the other good news is that organizations can do a lot to enable them to do just that.

Many companies have done a great deal to develop their peoples' levels of expertise in those areas in which the firm seeks to be the best. In fact, it is not uncommon to associate certain kinds of expertise with specific companies. For example, when you think of expertise in brand management, might P&G come to mind? When you think about quality and process improvement, would Toyota likely be up there on most people's lists? Are there specific kinds of expertise that are associated with, Apple, Merck, or GE? The same question could be asked about a lot of companies, maybe even your own.

With the fast paced change of today's world, gaining expertise and experience often requires novel approaches. For example training and education, which is always part of the expertise building formula, may have to be done in unusual or non-traditional ways. We are not just referring to different methods, like E-learning vs. classroom instruction, or university programs vs. internal courses. We are suggesting that you consider the extent that you are venturing outside your own organization's normal channels for expertise-building opportunities. Are your people able to increase their capabilities by working side by side with or taking courses offered by customers or suppliers? Are they challenged to do original research or able to bring in outside experts from whom they can learn. Are they encouraged to visit and learn from companies in different industries when appropriate, or for that matter work with people in different divisions within your own company? Developing and maintaining expertise is hard work, and it often requires original approaches to learning.

Of course, people do not develop deep expertise simply from educational experiences. It also comes from the discoveries made while directly applying what is being learned. So, do you give people the opportunity to try new things or to put what they are learning into practice? Are they able to have enough experiences to become more precise about what doesn't work, as well as what does? Part of expertise is *knowing that what you know, actually works the way you think it should!* Toss that comment around in your head for a minute.

Two Key Questions

If you aspire to build an organization of people who are willing and able to step up and challenge the ways things have always been done and produce growth, there are two very crucial questions that you need to be carefully addressing. Let's examine each of them.

The first question focuses on expertise: What specific expertise do you or others need to have in order to grow the business, effect change and accomplish something worthy going forward?

When AT&T was a regulated monopoly, it had people with exceptional expertise around tariff filings with the FCC and state Public Utility Commissions. That expertise was vital, because those filings were cumbersome and costly, and they had real consequences on the company's ability to grow and invest. But as the company moved further and further away from regulation and more and more into market driven competition, it wasn't able to identify and develop the right expertise needed to become a market leader or even sustain reasonable profits. (At the time of this writing, AT&T had already merged its wireless business with Cingular and had recently been acquired by SBC.)

To conquer a 70-foot wave, Laird Hamilton needed expertise in surfing, not negotiating or salesmanship. However, if he had worked in a large company and needed to get approval to use a Jet Ski, convince another group to provide him with one, and then had to beg other people for the time and funding to go attempt to ride the unridden realm, those latter skills may have come in very handy.

People need to possess in-depth knowledge about the areas they are attempting to build and grow. Don't make the too-common mistake of trying to inspire others to conceive some innovative change or new growth opportunity, and at the same time turn a blind eye to the expertise they need to be successful. And if the strategic success of your business in the future is going to be based on competencies that you do not currently have, you had better start attacking them—right now.

Once those future capabilities are determined, you must confront the second important question. Question Two is this: what kind of experiences must people have in order to quickly and fully develop the competencies required for ongoing success?

Those experiences must be meaningful and focused on the future, not just convenient or easy to provide.

Several years ago it was not uncommon to come across companies who stated that a significant chunk of their continuing growth was predicated upon international expansion. They were committed to opening new markets across the world, where it made sense for them. Yet, in some situations, the executives who had become responsible for their company's international operations were clueless. And why shouldn't they be, as they had never had any kind of experiences to prepare them for their new world order. (Believe it or not, we came across a few who after a couple of years in position still not did even possess a passport.) Even those with limited experience quickly discovered that adding a production plant and opening a new market in Asia proved to be entirely different than doing the same in Salt Lake City or Austin.

Today, many organizations seem to struggle in identifying the right kinds of developmental experiences for people that will lead to increased expertise. Think about it. Would you expect someone to be able to effectively lead a multi-business organization if he or she has always been given assignments in a single line of business? Would you expect groundbreaking innovation to occur in an organization where people have always worked at simply maintaining, preserving or at best incrementally improving what already exists? How would they acquire the knowledge needed for success?

It is also fascinating to still see the past vs. future focused experiences that some companies look for in recruiting new people. If you believe, for example, that innovation is the key to profitable growth and advantage in the banking industry, why would you continue to only recruit people with multiple years of banking? Yet many do, even though the people they hire have not been associated with a novel idea in their entire careers. The same recruitment blinders hold true for many industries, not just financial services. We wonder what would happen if companies who wanted to beef up innovation started opening their doors for some people from Disney Imagineering, Apple, edgy ad agencies or creative design firms.

When assessing the breadth and depths of competence that currently exists within your organization, there is one important note to keep in mind. Do not assume a person's expertise and experiences are directly tied to his or her current job responsibility. You may have tremendous levels of knowledge and capability that you simply know nothing about, because they have not yet been discovered or inventoried. Gail Mayville's background and experiences in recycling on a farm may not have even been considered relevant (or even necessary to know about) for a job as an administrative assistant. Yet the breakthrough idea that she was able to conceive because of that background certainly made a lasting difference for Ben & Jerry's. Be mindful that a person's HR profile or resume seldom tells the whole story.

Actions to Consider

Growing your organization requires you to have people who are capable and willing to challenge today's accepted ways and means and create breakthroughs that provide you with a sustainable advantage. To help develop more organizational competence, here are some actions you can begin working on right now.

- Recognize and accept that people who will take on the challenge to create growth must have competence—relevant expertise and experience.

- Learn more about your people. What gifts and talents do they already possess that can open new opportunities both today and tomorrow.

- Provide people with honest feedback about their current levels of competence—what they do well, what they need to improve, and what they do to excess. Be candid with them.

- Establish continuous learning as a desired organizational value. Push it, recognize it, and compensate it. Growth, be it individual or organizational, cannot occur without learning.

- Spend time discussing and deciding on the areas of expertise that are vital to your enterprise (or department) going forward, including those you currently do not have. Make them organizational imperatives and create measurable targets around them. (Keep the number relatively small and manageable.)

- Determine the experiences people must have to get smarter. Find ways to surface a number of novel alternatives and exciting possibilities for consideration.

- Allow people to "experience." Provide opportunities for them to experiment and test and tinker and reflect and tinker some more. Create simulators for them to practice in.

- Recruit people with expertise and experiences you need, not just the ones you are most familiar with.

- Stay invested in the outcome of building competence. Make sure people are convinced about its importance. Be closely involved in their education and experiences. Inspire and challenge them to make themselves smarter and better. Set goals around development.

To help further develop your own repertoire of experiences, here are some additional suggestions you personally can begin to immediately act upon.

- Volunteer to become part of entirely new assignments. Get involved with things you know very little about in order to get you hands on different things.

- Follow the sage advice of the local New Yorker who when asked by the visitors how to get to Carnegie Hall, answered, "practice, practice, practice." Work at your craft. Find ways to use your skills more frequently and in different ways.
- Align yourself with others who have more, wider or different experiences. Take advantage of and learn from what others already know how to do.
- Make tinkering a formal part of your growth. Give yourself and others on your team permission and resources to experiment. You need to determine what doesn't work as well as what does. Log in or journal what you learn so you can reflect on the lessons. This will also enable you to share lessons learned with others.
- Set a couple of stretch goals that will force you to try (and learn from) different approaches.
- Experiment in some fun ways. Go with friends and try ordering food that you have never eaten before. Rent a movie that you know nothing about. Visit a foreign country where you do not speak the language.
- Seek out a non-traditional next position in your career. Look to move outside of your silo, your discipline or even your current physical setting if feasible.
- Get to know people who work in different parts of your organization and see the world differently. Listen to their points of views. Ask for their help and opinions.
- Spend some time working beside a key customer or supplier in his or her environment. Experience what they experience in their everyday work life and in their dealings with you.

SELF-ASSURANCE

Achieving growth is hard work. It requires the willingness to challenge conventional wisdom (the way we have always done things) and the perseverance to initiate and lead changes that might not rest well with other people. What it ultimately takes is looking yourself in the eye, and deciding that you are going to go for it, knowing full well that there will be hazards along the way.

Jim Bonaminio is an individual we came upon that has a fair share of self-assurance. Jim is the founder and Big Cheese of an amazing enterprise in Fairfield, Ohio. Called Jungle Jims, it is a 310,000-square-foot international market, where you can buy almost anything imaginable in food products, and a whole lot of other items as well. At the Jungle a $2 bottle of wine sits comfortably next to one costing $2,000. "Aspiring chefs" learn to prepare fabulous dishes in Jim's cooking school, wine tasters sip imported merlots while eating exotic cheeses, and vegetarians graze in a 30,000 square foot produce area munching on any fruit or vegetable imaginable. Suffice it to say that Jungle Jim's has a legendary reputation in the southwest Ohio region.

Perhaps more than being an international market, Jungle Jim's is an idea factory. His team is always tinkering and trying new things to grow the business. The people there may sometimes feel like they are trying to change too much. But they are constantly in motion in order to find better and better ways to serve their customers. To that end, they are underway in the building of a second facility more centrally located in Cincinnati.

In our minds Jim does not aspire to be the biggest, richest or most powerful business baron in the world. But he does enjoy playing the game of business, and he continually demonstrates the confidence that he will win enough pots to stay in the game for a long time. He knows that many ideas will not be rousing successes, but that does not make him afraid to keep trying. That said, is their new 70,000 square foot property a huge risk? You bet. Can he tell you exactly what kind of a place it will be? Not when we last saw him. Will it succeed? We would bet on it.

We learned some fascinating things about Jim that likely contributed to the self-assurance we see in him and his associates. From his early childhood, he has always figured out a way to make money, not always a great deal, but often more than enough. As a kid he picked and sold cattails to people for a dollar a pop, as a means of keeping bugs away. He negotiated a deal with the mayor of his town where he was given permission to paint addresses on the new curbs—for donations only. He averaged about fifty cents a house and made more in a day than many local factory-working fathers made in a week. On another occasion, he bought the oversupply of potatoes from local farmers and sold them off the back of an old truck. He has always found a way to play the game and make enough to play another round.

By the way, it may surprise you to learn that Jim's associates will tell you he does not think "out of the box," the well-used attribute frequently associated with people who challenge the status quo. Then they tell you the punch line—that Jim does not believe in the box to begin with. Whether or not we care to admit it, most of us find comfort inside the boxes of our lives and feel remarkably inspired when we have the guts to break out of them on occasions. Jungle Jim has the confidence to live, and the courage to act, in the free-flowing, unpredictable, ever changing world all the time.

Growth leaders like Jim have a rational belief in themselves and their abilities. They are neither haphazard nor foolish. Instead they are aware of what they are attempting to do and the consequences (both good and bad) of their actions. They possess an enhanced internal strength that comes from confidence and courage, the two attributes that make up self-assurance.

Confidence is more than a set of convincing words. It is even more than a belief. It is knowledge about yourself that comes from your abilities. You can tell people all day that you are confident you can win the sale, figure out the software glitch or increase your profit by 15 percent. But if those are only empty words to make you appear capable to others, when you actually feel completely inadequate, lost, or downright terrified, you will have a real struggle on your hands. Being confident does not ensure that you will always be successful. But it does provide you with the knowledge that you can be. And that knowledge is crucial for tackling things that have never been done before.

Courage has humorously been defined as that thing we wish we had more of when we really needed it! On one hand it can be viewed as a self-generated source of power. On the other, it is an asset that many are fearful about relying on. Think about it. Courage is generally needed in risky situations. And it is a pretty safe bet that when you are attempting to change something or to put forth an innovative idea for growth, risk will be involved. Your physical safety is hopefully not on the line, but never forget that your reputation likely is.

Courage requires you to test yourself, to determine what you are really made of. Therefore, it should come as no surprise that the root word of courage is the French word that means heart. It simply takes a lot of heart to act with courage, especially when your logical mind is screaming at you to just play it safe. That is why it is so inspiring to hear or read about people who have exemplified great courage. Just keep in mind that it is often easier to read about someone else's courage than it is to muster it up yourself.

Over the next few chapters, you will have the opportunity to look inside yourself and understand your own level of self-assurance. What are your levels of confidence and courage? Are confidence and courage personal assets in your individual growth? Are confidence and courage part of your company's internal character? We hope you will examine what you are doing to strengthen confidence and courage in those whom you are asking to take risks.

Chapter 10: Feeling Unstoppable: Confidence

Jim Cramer is one of the world's top financial gurus and most entertaining television personalities. He is the host of the daily, financial education show called "Smart Money." What a blast it is to watch or listen to "Cramer" spout off passionately about a stock no one has heard of or even considered investing in. With props in hand, Jim is presenting his pitch to you personally in a maniacal and convincing manner. And you are spellbound—not only by the financial information but also by the hysterical and "easy to understand" way it is presented. By the time he has finished his tirade, you've been sold and you are rearranging your account with Smith Barney to buy the stock. He has transferred his confidence in this company to you. You see, Jim Cramer, doesn't believe he can make you money, he knows he can make you richer.

Great athletes exude confidence. They fully expect to win every time they compete. Conversely, the good athletes want to convince you and themselves that they can win. You can just see it as the competition unfolds. It is the body language, the facial expressions, the tentative follow-through on the back hand, the "short-arming" of the free-throw or the double toe loop instead of the triple.

Think back on some of the world class athletes of this century's first decade. When Roger Federer strolls to center court, Michelle Kwan poises to begin her long program on the ice, or Tiger Woods steps up to the first tee box, each of them expects to finish at the top. This is not an impossible dream or mental pep talk, it is the inevitable outcome. They knew they could beat whoever they were competing against, and their individual opponents knew it as well. Good athletes believe they can win. Great athletes know they will win. Think about the advantage that provides.

The advantage of confidence is not limited to athletes. It is one of the factors that allows world class sales people, innovation teams, surgeons and individuals in any vocation to outperform others who also possess extraordinary talent.

Former leaders at Bank One certainly understand the importance of confidence to an organization's success. The bank's history can be traced back to the holding company, First Bancgroup of Ohio. The flagship bank of City National Bank was combined with several other Ohio banks and eventually renamed Bank One (the holding company became Banc One Corporation). Its business model was called the "uncommon partnership" which was the decentralization of all decision-making to affiliate banks. All executives, managers and employees pledged their allegiance to the "uncommon partnership." CEO John B. McCoy had touted the strategy as the way to grow the business and stay close to the customer. But, with the beginning of interstate banking, Bank One's reach extended beyond the Ohio borders. And the merger and acquisition stampede accelerated the Bank's position from sleepy City National Bank in Columbus, Ohio to the sixth largest Bank in the U.S. By the mid-1990's, it was also clear that growth through acquisition was out of control. Due to higher infrastructure and integration costs, the Bancorp began experiencing adverse financial results. McCoy and his chief advisors decided it was time to unravel the "uncommon partnership" and develop a line-of-business strategy. To introduce this change, McCoy decided to invite all the top leaders of the bank to a summit in Atlanta.

McCoy understood the devastating impact this decision would have on the fiercely independent, sales leaders in each affiliate. However, lower profits, movement of sales leaders to support M&A integration and excessive turnover thinned the "A" player ranks at the bank. Atlanta was to be a morale booster and a reenlisting of the top performers in the Bank's future. But, what it turned out to be was an event that created a crisis of confidence in senior leadership. As the CEO began to preview the new line-of-business model, McCoy made it clear that certain people in the conference room would not be with the Bank in the future. Instead of raising the inspiration level, McCoy crushed the hopes and beliefs in the future. Confidence was replaced by cynicism. It was clear that senior management didn't have the "big company" experience to lead this transformation effectively. Ultimately, McCoy was replaced by Jamie Dimon, a former senior executive of Citigroup. His initial action was to invest personally in the bank's future. His message to all employees—we will turn this company around.

Nothing succeeds like confidence. When you are truly and justifiably confident, it radiates from you like sunlight, and attracts success to you like a magnet. George Bush did not radiate confidence in his public speaking skills. This is why his followers were "shaking in their boots" prior to each debate with John Kerry. Self-confidence is an important factor in most emotional intelligence decisions:

- Am I talented enough to be successful at this job?
- Am I enthusiastic about the role that I am playing?
- Am I capable of persuading people to my point-of-view?
- Will people be motivated to follow me?

What is Confidence?

Confidence is more than an attitude, it is an attribute. It comes from having a clear personal vision and an understanding of how you're going to set sail. It comes from acting with integrity. It comes from a strong sense of purpose and personal values. It comes from a strong commitment to take responsibility, rather than just let life happen. Confidence is a vital element of risk-taking and innovation. It is about knowing that you have what it takes for success to occur. With confidence, success is not only anticipated, it is expected. This confidence then motivates all the hard work to achieve the final result.

As a leader, it's so important to know yourself. If you know that all things are possible—no circumstances can derail you. Process challenging happens because people understand that change, growth, and improvement are inevitable and important. This attitude keeps people searching for the answers. It all ends up with the innovation occurring, the company growing and the people (employees and customers) engaged. And your confidence has been the fuel behind it.

Why is confidence such a powerful tool in risk-taking? There is a "believability" aspect to confidence. People "believe" they can accomplish the difficult assignment. This believability is attached more to the overall talent of the person rather than the depth of experience. Because a person is highly skilled, some individuals, teams and companies will jump on the "believe train." However, they may soon become disenchanted because believing is different than knowing. Knowing is a higher level of confidence.

Knowing people have both talent and experience. They have been there before, and have accomplished the feat. These people know that they can challenge and create change. Their associates understand this "knowing confidence" and accept risk-taking as an every day part of the success menu. Confidence is knowing you can do it, knowing that you are capable of accomplishing anything you want, and knowing this from the first minute that you started down the path. It is not arrogance. Arrogance is born out of fear and insecurity. Confidence comes from strength and integrity.

A Profile in Confidence

Erik Weihenmayer thought his life was over at age 13. He slowly became blind from a disease called retinoschisis. It unraveled Erik's retinas and left him totally blind at the beginning of his high school years. After a few years of denial and pity parties, Erik came to grips with his new situation and decided to really live life with what he had.

So, he decided to step out—way out—and learn how to mountain climb. He had no experience mountain climbing when he was sighted. Now, he was going to conquer this difficult sport without his sight. The impetus was a letter sent to him in Braille by a school for blind children. This group wanted to experiment taking blind children rock climbing. Erik grasped the group's vision and made a personal commitment to learn the sport.

As he embraced the challenge, he built confidence through practice and unleashing his other senses. In an interview on "The Hour of Power," Erik told Robert A. Schuller that "when I got up there on the rock, and I felt the pattern of the sun on the rock, and the textures of the rock, and the sound of space as I got really high up, these beautiful sound vibrations moving through space, I just thought this is beautiful. I just realized that the adventure of my life wasn't over."

At the age of 32, Weihenmayer achieved the pinnacle of climbing success by reaching the top of Mt. Everest. But, this became only the first stanza of a remarkable song of life that Eric is experiencing. In 2003, he completed the Climbing Blind: Tibet Expedition where he led six blind Tibetan teenagers to a 23,000-foot peak just North of Mt. Everest. On the Climbing Blind Tibet Expedition 2004 Website, Weihenmayer reflected on the expedition.

"I'm starting to put it all into perspective. Why did we think it would be a good idea to take inexperienced blind Tibetan teens into a tough, cold, and hostile environment? I think about a dispatch I wrote before we left: 'Strength, courage, and resiliency are part of most every person's character; we just need the opportunity to bring it out.' Looking back, I would revise that statement slightly: Strength, courage and resiliency may be in everyone, but they start as a tiny spark and it's only through facing challenges that they grow and blaze into the force that directs our lives and ultimately creates change in the world."

Why do you think the Tibetan children followed Erik Weihenmayer? Why did they have confidence in him? Why did they lean their heads on his shoulder when they became weary? He was walking in their world. He had experienced the darkness and hopelessness of life. But, his strength and courage allowed him to overcome the denial and to forge ahead with his life. He had climbed Mt. Everest. Just imagine the emotions of other blind people when they heard about Erik's successful feat. It opened up new vistas for theirs lives. Impossibility became a possibility. Believing now became knowing. "And this man is going to lead me to the top of a 23,000-foot mountain peak." Their confidence was the force that allowed them to endure tough, difficult times.

Anything can be achieved through focused, determined effort, commitment and self-confidence.

Traditionally, confidence is defined as "trust in" or "reliance upon". When you have self-confidence, you trust in, or rely upon, yourself or the people with you. Possessing confidence in yourself means knowing that you have the ability to become or achieve whatever you want. This expectation drives the success of most entrepreneurs. They have worked hard to build the self-confidence for the diligent effort needed to build a business.

Think about people you have met who are "magnetic." A magnetic person is someone who literally radiates confidence. They exude certainty, assurance and charisma. They have a strong sense of security; a feeling that, no matter what happens people can count on them to make decisions and take action in a manner that produces an acceptable outcome. Look around your organization. Is there a sense of certainty, assurance and positive arrogance in the company? Is the senior leadership demonstrating the swagger that says "we know that we're on the right growth track?" Has senior leadership supported middle management and shown confidence in them?

Confidence is magnetic, powerful and profound. It's the calm voice amidst the chaos. It's the firm hand on your shoulder when you're lost in a crowd. It's what legends and leaders are made of. Can't you clearly see Erik Wiehenmayer providing stability and assurance with the six blind, Tibetan blind children on their treacherous journey?

What Confidence Isn't

One of the primary reasons why self-confidence is such a rare quality is because most people believe one or more of the following three common misconceptions:

Misconception 1: Confidence is a by-product of exceptional knowledge, beauty, experience and talent.

Confidence is not merely a by-product of exceptional knowledge, beauty, experience or talent. Confidence is about faith, trust, and belief. How many times have you seen, known or heard about the beautiful, talented, successful individual who is painfully or even self-destructively insecure? Despite their natural gifts, these individuals lack basic trust or belief in themselves.

Misconception 2: Confidence is not something that you can learn or develop; you have it or you don't.

If there is one thing humans are, it's infinitely adaptable. Physical therapists talk about the soldiers wounded in Iraq. Many have lost a limb or limbs and do not have the ability to move or feel portions of their bodies. Yet, with help and perseverance, they were able to learn new ways of moving and functioning. Despite the fact that they had done things (i.e. writing with their right hand) for decades, they were able to learn new methods of accomplishing the same things (writing with their left hand or in some cases, using their mouth) in a matter of weeks or months. Confidence, too, can be learned.

Misconception 3: Your level of confidence is directly aligned with the amount of validation, praise or recognition you receive.

While praise and validation certainly help people feel good about themselves, these are by nature transient, conditional things, and therefore not a reliable way to sustain one's self-confidence.

Confidence is about knowing that winning is possible. As the leader, it is about when you tell someone that you have confidence in him or her, you are saying, "I believe in you. I know you can lead us." Even if they have no prior record of accomplishing whatever it is you know they can accomplish.

Confidence at Fox News Channel

Fox News Channel is an interesting case study of the impact confidence can have in achieving business success. Launched on October 7, 1996, the network quickly rose from ten million households to 85 million subscribers in early 2005. A brash, confident Roger Ailes was hired by Rupert Murdoch, CEO and major shareholder of News Corporation to start the network. Ailes had experienced life very differently than most media executives. He started his career as a ditch digger and moved quickly into a political consulting role. His work with Richard Nixon gained him national notoriety. Searching for new opportunities, Ailes left the political consulting world and invested his last dollar into a failed Broadway production. This foray into unchartered waters found him returning to what he knew best—the news media.

Murdoch engaged Ailes in starting up Fox News Channel. He took the challenge realizing that assignment to take on CNN and MSNBC would be difficult. Ailes remembered that "we had no studios, no programs, no talent, no ideas, no news-gathering capabilities, weak stations in news, no history of news. And we had tough competitors. So, it was a daunting task. And we had no distribution."

But, from day one, Ailes and his team had confidence. They knew what Fox News would look and feel like. This confidence was passed on to every new hire. Jack Abernathy joined the Fox News team as the Chief Financial Officer. "I knew we could come in here and create a credible news service at a fraction of the cost that people had expected," he said. Neil Cavuto, the top-notch business anchor moved to Fox News from CNBC because of Ailes and the opportunity. "I really liked Roger and felt he was an exciting guy to work for."

In early 1998, the turning point for Fox News occurred. They had the confidence and courage to take on the O.J. Simpson and Bill Clinton stories. While the other networks failed to seize the moment, Fox approached both stories with "fair and balanced" coverage. Simpson, Lewinski and the 2000 election coverage from Florida put Fox News in American homes to stay. Fox News had the confidence to dare to be different. Playing defense is not part of their game plan. This is why they became the #1 news channel on cable.

To sustain the confidence in leadership, Ailes worked hard at keeping information flowing. Like most great leaders, he communicated openly about the business, and this kept employees connected to the enterprise. The problem with leaders who aren't open to dialogue with their staff, Ailes said, is fear. "A leader who does not fear making a decision naturally has no fear of openness. I might make a counter call, because I'm relying on my own experience, or because there are factors they don't know about, but I'll listen to everybody and then I'll say 'No, let's do it this way and I'll take the consequences of that.'"

Roger Ailes knows that as a leader he was responsible for the cornerstone of confidence at Fox News. That gives one a foundation to stand on and turn the business loose.

Confidence Makes the Difference

Can you remember back to your childhood and your experience in learning how to ride a bike? Your parents encouraged you and even gave you some instructions. You were just a bit petrified, but you knew that your best friend has been riding for two weeks. You fell off the bike over and over again, but you maintained your confidence about the final result. Mom, Dad and your friends kept encouraging you by saying, "you'll get it the next time. You almost have it." The confidence in your ability to accomplish something that you had never done before drove you to grab the bicycle and start all over again. In the back of your mind, failure was understood, but it really never became an option. You had confidence in yourself. You were going to ride the bicycle.

Over the years, we have facilitated numerous team development and strategy sessions with various companies. One aspect of each session has generally been true. By the end of a meeting, we would have a true sense as to whether the team would win or lose. The determining factor was most frequently the manager. In the worst cases, the manager had been unable to demonstrate confidence for the team, confidence in the team's plan and confidence in the team's approach to execution. Think about the consequences of that, given that a business's growth hinges on the manager's ability to convince the team about their ability to succeed.

In these sessions, we loved to watch how the great leaders would go on "search and rescue" missions looking for overboard employees. The leader's confidence was the "lifeboat" that revived positive thinking and an employee's belief that climbing back on board was the right thing to do.

Many employees are "fence sitters" at work today. Abandoning ship is not their preferred strategy, but confidence in their leader to steer the ship in the right direction is low. They are diligently watching for any sign that will move them off the fence and encourage their belief in the leader's course. But, the messages received are often like this one:

> *"All RMs, team leads, and sales managers need to have logged on at least one call from this week or next into CRM by next Friday. NO EXCEPTIONS.*
>
> *We are being stacked-ranked against other divisions, and we need to be at the top of the list. Our division CEO is under pressure, which puts me under pressure, which puts you under pressure.*
>
> *Anybody not getting this done will be attending a mandatory, lengthy, extremely boring CRM supplemental training session to be scheduled at a very undesirable location --- maybe on the weekend."*

Do you think a message like this could ever motivate anyone to sprint out and become actively engaged in the business? What is a manager thinking about when delivering such a message? Growth accelerates when the leader is able to transfer her confidence to each employee. When this happens, business plans become real and achievable.

Building an environment of confidence is an important job of senior leadership. Business growth will be lackluster if the employee base believes leadership lacks credibility and if leadership is unsuccessful in creating confidence in their plan. Sadly, there are managers who are not effective in accomplishing either of these. For some reason, leadership has not envisioned the payoff in developing their personal leadership brand with middle management, first line supervisors, new management associates and the rank and file. Business growth ultimately comes down to the level of confidence the employees have in the leadership.

As employee confidence expands and leadership credibility improves, the far horizons of business success come into focus and employees are ready to move forward. And the conquering of these horizons sends companies on extended growth spurts.

Building Individual Confidence—*Reflection Questions*

After reading this chapter, you should understand the importance of personal confidence in building businesses and careers. Here are some questions for you to assess your current state of personal confidence: Do not underestimate how important this attribute is on your ability to successfully create new opportunities for challenge and growth.

1. What level of confidence do I have that I can deliver the expectations in my current position? What areas of my position am I uneasy about? Do I demonstrate confidence to my direct reports and peers?

2. As I shape my career, what must I work on to raise my confidence level and project confidence to people who work with me?

3. What is my plan to build personal confidence? (Think about the different characteristics defined in the previous chapters.) Which one(s) will allow me to build higher levels of confidence?

4. Who will help me monitor progress in this area?

Growing the Business—*Executive Reflection*

1. As you work with people in the company, do you sense the level of confidence needed to "grow the business?" Do you see the "swagger" needed to compete today in your industry? Expand on your answer.

2. What actions are you taking to raise the confidence level of employees and improve the leadership team's credibility?

3. What is preventing you, as senior leaders, in building employee confidence? Why are you not making the investment?

4. Assess the confidence level of your important business units across the company. What are the top three issues lowering confidence levels in the company? How does the senior team raise the confidence level in the company?

Chapter 11: The Heart of the Matter: Courage

Cowardly Lion: Courage! What makes a king out of a slave? Courage! What makes a flag on the mast to wave? Courage! What makes the elephant charge his tusk in the misty mist, or the dusky dusk? What makes the muskrat guard his musk? Courage! What makes the sphinx the seventh wonder? Courage! What makes the dawn come up like thunder? Courage! What makes the Hottentot so hot? What puts the "ape" in the apricot? What have they got that I ain't got?

Dorothy, Scarecrow, Tin woodsman: Courage!

Cowardly Lion: You can say that again! Huh?

Courage. Lewis and Clarke had it as they left St. Louis to explore the great unknown of the Pacific Northwest. The only thing that was certain for these explorers was what success would look like—The Pacific Ocean. But, everything between St. Louis and the Pacific Ocean could be termed a mystery. It was the mystery that attracted these brave leaders and their team to tackle this significant assignment. Their courage unlocked a whole new world of discovery for adventurous Americans. It was an action that contributed to America's greatness.

Courage. Alan Shepard had it on May 5, 1961. The rigorous training schedule was complete. No more skill development or additional experiences were required for this assignment. Years of sweat equity, commitment and perseverance brought him to the launch pad on this Spring morning. As a Navy test pilot, Alan Shepard had been closely associated with "risk-taking." His job was to test the limits. But, this morning was different. He was being launched where no other American had ever been before—space. The commander was thrust into an adventure by a Redstone rocket on a ballistic trajectory suborbital flight—a flight which carried him to an altitude of 116 statute miles and to a landing point 302 statute miles down the Atlantic Missile

Range. Shepard's experience and skills prepared him for the flight. It gave him the confidence to climb into the capsule. *It was his courage that helped him shut the capsule door.*

Courage. Our brave troops have it in Iraq as they search buildings and open doors not knowing what awaits them on the other side. It is a treacherous mystery. But, courage keeps them pursuing the enemy into unfamiliar space. It is their duty in the quest for freedom.

Courage. Mark Michon had it as he joined Fifth Third Bank's Western Michigan Affiliate in 2003 as the Executive Vice President of the Investment Advisors line of business (Trust, Securities, wealth building services for customers). It was his job to grow the investment business—not tomorrow, but right now.

Michon was recruited into a difficult situation. The Western Michigan Affiliate (formerly Old Kent Bank) had just recently been acquired by Fifth Third Bank, headquartered in Cincinnati. The M&A integration and the uncertainty about Fifth Third's culture was the impetus for an 18 percent turnover in IA professionals. The core group remaining embraced a transaction culture which rewarded sales not relationships. This strategy would achieve short-term revenue projections but was not the customer-focused approach needed to grow a business long-term. He was told that any strategy beyond "what did you sell today" was irrelevant. Michon decided to embark on a frontier journey that would provide each professional the courage to change and to build a personal commitment to the bank.

In 2004, Michon began architecting the vision for Investment Advisers (IA) in Western Michigan. Why go to the frontier? He was convinced that having a shared vision and set of values would support teamwork, would create an environment consistent with the team's personal values and would communicate a common message of what IA wanted to represent to the clients and the communities being served by Fifth Third. As he started writing the vision, he talked with key members of the team about the importance of a clear vision and a set of core values. Their energy and excitement fueled Mark's development work.

After attending a leadership retreat, Michon finalized his thoughts about the group's vision and values. He introduced the work at various meetings and listened to all the feedback. These sessions generated some new thoughts and allowed Michon to strengthen the vision because it was now shared. To seal the deal, Mark had the courage to start promoting vision and values as the key to business growth. His entire staff attended a one-day seminar entitled—Living Your Values. The session was so impactful that members of his team promoted the program to their customers. The IA professionals also discovered that their values were aligned with their leader and the organization. This gave them the confidence and courage to start developing customer relationships instead of pursuing a transaction-based revenue life. And they even handed out their vision and values booklets to their clients.

Michon was convinced that the commitment to vision and values had been a major factor is IA's recent success—reduction in employee turnover, increase in customer retention and increases in revenue and profitability. Even more important, IA had experienced greater cama-raderie and internal relationship building, commitment to the success of each team member and greater comfort level (trust) for candid dia-logue between leadership and staff. Top internal talent joined the IA team because of the leadership environment.

Mark had one final stroke of courage. He decided to share the team's vision and values statement with Fifth Third's corporate leaders. Michon had been advised that "Cincinnati wouldn't really care about a vision statement," and he knew he was placing his reputation on the line by taking this approach. To Michon's delight, he received a three-word message from the corporate leader of IA affirming the team's work—"I like it."

What Lewis and Clark, Alan Shepard, Mark Michon, our US fight-ing forces and other business growth leaders all understand is that suc-cess is measured in hundreds of small steps across the momentum equation. Courage is required to take each small step. Growth leaders know that vision sets the stage, passion moves you to the starting line, and courage makes progress happen.

So, how do you demonstrate courage in your work? How could

having more courage in your work lead to professional and business growth? Is there anything that you will risk it all for? Do you have the courage to even think about "risking it all?" Or is financial security your "true North?"

Where is the Courage

There is a real paradox blooming in corporate America today. And it is causing personal conflict and anxiety at many levels in organizations. The paradox is associated with an employee's beliefs and their unwillingness to step up and hold fast to their vision and values in the face of adversity. It is easier or more convenient to back off and go along with the pack. Our stamina for what we believe in fritters away under our absence of courage. Randy Melville, Vice President of Urban and Ethnic Marketing at PepsiCo, refers to adversity "as an opportunity to reveal your character." Many employees and managers fail this test.

What is startling to us is that even people in firms with "leadership reputations" have acquiesced. We asked the question recently to a group of young leaders from a principled, growth-oriented company with an outstanding reputation of being a "great place to work." We wanted to know "why it is difficult to have courage in the workplace." The response heard most often was that "I am not ready to leave the company or to be put on the back burner. I just can't trust my boss to respond in the right way." Such principled statements make us shake our heads and wonder what it will take for corporate America to ever experience a real growth era again.

We have worked with several senior teams who do not develop trust and consequently, have lower levels of courage. At the top of the pyramid, the practice is to share information and to review goals and strategies. Courageous exchanges are not part of the terrain. CEOs, Presidents and Senior Managers are not interested in being second-guessed. Questions are met with defensive stares. They bounce off a stern veneer and smack the questioner right between the eyes. The staffer gets the message—"Don't take me on. I know what is best. I've been doing this longer than you. And by the way, I am the boss." Courage throughout the organization is extinguished in one brief interaction.

No courage at the senior level is a precursor for a *courageless* environment on the production line, in the research center and on the front lines. Without courage, innovation and risk-taking have little chance to thrive or survive in the company. This means **No Growth**. It becomes a stagnant working place with mediocre performers. And the company will struggle every quarter to achieve growth expectations.

In our experiences we have found that a number of senior managers possess large egos. We have even come across some that literally kiss the mirror every morning before they walk out of their palatial mansions and leave for the office, proclaiming to everyone around them, "I am what success looks like." With this view of life, engaging these people in questioning and reassessment of strategy is not a career enhancer for those posing the questions. This worldview has diminished the appetite for innovation throughout the company. The absence of modeling courage at the top is a threat to the future existence of corporate America, shareholder value and the development of outstanding business leaders.

Just as individual and companies need courage, countries must make difficult decisions about their future as well. Consider the turmoil in early 2006 in France and their unwillingness to address cultural peculiarities which have created economic stagnation. A new law designed to make labor markets more competitive provoked student riots. But, for decades, France had been the country of lifetime employment, the country where almost every citizen's dream was to be a civil servant, the country where work was 35 hours per week and where the vacation benefit started at six weeks a year. The passion seemed to be for status quo; business growth was not wanted. So, solutions were not presented because there were none. Arrogance was winning. Many observers of this situation in France were saying that the country was on the verge of disaster.

Passion and Courage

Without passion for change, courage exits the scene. Passion breathes life into courage. "Passionless" people neither feel courage nor act in a courageous manner. They have left their heart and soul in the past. They are somewhere else. Please understand this—without passion, courage doesn't exist. And courage moves people to higher levels of commitment. And commitment moves mountains. And mountains are conquered by ideas. This is why companies must create work environments where peoples' passion leads to the courage necessary to stand up for what they believe in.

What does the company and the leader earn by pursuing passion and courage? Honest dialogue, breakthrough ideas, staff retention and corporate growth are some immediate outcomes. When you stimulate passion in your organization and convince people to love their work, courage will flourish. It will break down the walls of complacency. The ideas will multiply and growth will return. (This is another reason why we encourage you to find your passion!)

We live with managers every day in our work. We noticed that most managers are not anxious to promote courage as an admired characteristic. Courage may require confrontation. It will bring about uncomfortable situations. Courage looks you straight in the eye and says, "are you with me?" And too many of us say, "I have too much at stake to put what I believe on the line."

Leaders must begin the dialogue with their people about "talking and acting courageously." The first question should be, "what are you really passionate about in your job?" All bosses must clearly understand what turns their people on, that is, what people really care about. Passion is required in everyone's work. And it is the leader's obligation to understand their passions and insist that they pursue them.

In many environments, it takes courage for a leader to encourage people to go after something more than just the monthly number, or to find a more exciting, fulfilling way to deliver it. And it takes some real guts from the associates to be willing to accept that challenge, because there is risk associated with it. Yet, this must be done for the company, the shareholders and the firm's future leaders, because as the expression goes, "people do not achieve great things because they have to, but because they want to."

Actions for Senior Leaders

Senior Leaders in corporate America must be committed to allowing courage to emerge and be relevant in their organizations. In growth companies, leaders believe that courage is an integral part of the innovation equation. Although additional action ideas for increasing courage will be offered in the following chapter, here are some specific tactics that can be introduced by senior managers to stimulate courage in companies:

- Talk courageously about the future. Inspire all employees with a picture of an aggressive growth company. Let them know that it will take individual and team courage to achieve the vision. Help all employees see what a courageous organization looks like. Describe the environment. Spell it out.

- Introduce courage as a strategic part of the performance management process. Implore your employees to have courage in their work. Candidly assess their level of courage annually. Determine if the courage meter in your company is moving forward. If progress is stalled, figure out how to better utilize the performance management system to stimulate risk-taking.

- Share the "courage" stories from the annual performance process throughout the company. Find a creative way to introduce the stories—courage on courage. Help employees understand what the "stories" mean financially for the company.

- Publicly recognize all acts of courage. Let people witness the behavior you are seeking. Make the recognition worthwhile.

- Recruit "courage" into the organization. Request experienced recruiters to probe about acts of risk-taking in the candidate's current role. Evaluate this skill area prior to making a final employment offer. This will also send the recruit a message about your

company's "risk-taking" culture.
- Walk around observing courage taking place. Reinforce the behavior on the spot.

Some wonderful growth companies (Arthur Andersen, Enron, Tyco, WorldCom, etc.) have been toppled because courage was eschewed by senior leadership. Courage takes many forms—the mad scientist, the whistleblower, the intrapreneur, the brand manager, the research associate, the customer service representative. It doesn't matter what the size, shape or form, just encourage its life in your organization. Courage spurns inactivity and status quo thinking. It moves people to do the right thing for the company and themselves. Courage makes things happen.

Building Individual Courage—*Reflection Questions*

After reading this chapter, you should understand the importance of personal courage in building businesses and careers. Here are some questions for you to assess your current level of personal courage:

1. What is it you truly believe? What is it that you are passionate about?
2. Picture your passion. How would you describe it? How has it impacted your life? How has passion fueled courage in your work?
3. At what point will you not defend your passion? When will courage not surface and your beliefs are betrayed? Why will this occur?
4. Describe your reputation in the organization for "acting with courage." How have you displayed courage in the last 6 months?
5. What were the overall results and outcomes?
6. Can you describe why you may not act courageously? How do you respond when this happens?

Growing the Business—*Executive Reflection*

As senior leadership, you should understand the importance of personal courage in growing the business. Here are a series of questions for senior leadership to assess the current level of courage in the organization:

1. Over the past year, what percentage of your business growth can be attributed to new products or services? Are you satisfied with this number?

2. How often are you hearing about individual acts of courage in support of customers? Are employees taking risks for customers?

3. How is the company rewarding courage? Will these individuals believe the reward is worth the risk? What have the "high courage" people contributed to business growth?

4. What can the senior leadership group do to make courage part of the organizational culture?

5. To what extent is courage an important capability in the promotion package?

Chapter 12: Building Self-Assurance

Challenging current ways of doing things and instituting change to improve and ultimately grow a business can be frightening work. Think about it. The growth frontier is unexplored territory. There is the expression, "the pioneers get the arrows and the settlers get the land." Like the early pioneers, those who are seeking to discover new ways of doing things are going to run into unexpected hazards and encounter problems where the solutions have yet to be developed. Besides the great resources of commitment and competence, people need to have a healthy dose of self-assurance, the confidence and courage to proceed.

How prevalent are confidence and courage in your organization today? If we were to visit you, would we clearly see that people are acting with confidence in spite of all the uncertainty? Would we see people courageous enough to step up and make themselves vulnerable, by pursuing dreams or ideas that go against the grain? Would we see leaders modeling these attributes? Would we see them in you?

Earlier we referenced a survey called the *Characteristics of Admired Leaders*, where people have been asked to rate the seven attributes they most admire in leaders they would willingly choose to follow. Surprisingly, only 20 percent have selected courage in their top seven. More and more people we share this data with are surprised that it is so low. They comment about how great of a need there is for their organizational leaders to have courage, for a variety of obvious reasons. But when we ask about the level of courage they actually see demonstrated in their organizations, the anecdotal responses we receive indicate that courage is seldom a perceived strength of leaders—or others for that matter. So, if it is important or desired, why do only 20 percent select it?

The obvious answer is other attributes are just viewed as more important. The more subtle answer might be that too many organizational leaders reach high positions without showing much courage. On a day to day basis, maybe courage is just too great of an ideal to hope for. It does require a tremendous amount of effort, including the effort to focus on something more than just next quarter's earnings. It is clearly an identified cornerstone of the great world and historical leaders, but perhaps it is viewed as too much to expect from the organizational leaders with whom they come into contact at work.

Whether pushing for clean water around the world, introducing a radical new look for a very successful car, or moving friends and neighbors across the road to a dramatically improved quality of life, courage and confidence have always been key ingredients for moving a person's visions and desires forward. It is just not a safe bet to assume that people will step out into the risky, unsafe unknown without them.

So the question once again is what can be done to build or strengthen an individual's self-assurance. Although inspiring words can help, pep talks or motivational speakers are not the complete answer. For the most part, self-assurance is built through experience. The challenge is to provide people with experiences where they can be successful, learn to have faith in and rely on their talents and abilities, and to trust themselves more fully. They need to have experiences where their beliefs about who they are and what they can do are reinforced and strengthened. As we have said earlier, the success of mastering a 30-foot wave, provides the foundation for going after a 40 or even a 70-footer.

It is our guess that the passion and vision Candy Lightner had about eliminating drunk drivers gave her the fire to take on the laws and accepted customs of the land, related to drinking and driving. That fire was needed because she would encounter numerous setbacks and brick walls along the way. Yet, she continued to learn from her experiences, both successes and failures, and what may have started as impassioned idealism turned into rock solid self-assurance.

When attempting to strengthen self-assurance, never underestimate the importance of commitment and competence. Self-assurance comes from caring deeply about something. Would you willingly put yourself in harm's way, physically or emotionally, for something that is not real-ly important to you? By the same token, would you venture into dan-ger if you did not believe you were capable of dealing with whatever was dealt to you? The answer for both questions is likely "no."

Actions to Consider

For an organization to grow and survive, it must have people who have the courage and confidence to be innovative, and to put them-selves and their companies "out there." To help develop more self-assurance, here are some actions you can begin working on right now.

- Recognize and accept that people who will take on the challenge to create change must have commitment. They need to have a com-pelling reason to put themselves at risk.
- Take time to discuss "personal bests" with your people. Help them examine and learn from those times in their lives when they over-came great challenges and were successful.
- Make it safe for people to surface their fears or anxieties. Let them know that support is available and they are not alone. Whether trav-eling in a foreign country or making an important presentation, having others with you is usually very comforting—and helpful.
- Work with people to develop options. Choice can be very liberat-ing, and increase the level of confidence about potential success. Knowing that you have the choice to fall down in order to slow yourself when trying to ski a Black Diamond slope that is way beyond your ability, might give you the impetus (and feeling of safety) you need to give it a try.
- Spend time with your people. Listen to them. Encourage them. Give them a little rope. Recognize them when they succeed, espe-cially after taking a risk.
- Help people learn from mistakes and "get back on the horse." Let them see that they have the ability to bounce back from mistakes.
- Model courage. Show them that you are willing to put yourself in the crosshairs. Observing acts of courage can be very inspiring.

People will often say to themselves, "when I saw her willing to take that kind of risk, I knew I had to try."

- Have people plot their life lines, identifying the high and low points of their lives. Ask them to uncover the times when they felt most confident or courageous. Help them determine what they did to increase those feelings.

- Remember the concept of "small wins." Provide people with experiences where they can be successful. Then raise the level of challenge or difficulty a bit. Throwing people in the middle of the lake without a life-preserver to teach them to swim sounds harsh. But how certain can you be that, if they survive and make it to shore, they won't devote the rest of their lives to "getting even" with you for scaring the daylights out of them, instead of valuing their newly developed skill and courageously taking it to the next level.

- Foster teamwork and collaboration. Knowing you are part of a capable and trusting team inspires confidence. Destiny no longer falls entirely on your shoulders

- Allow your group to participate in a challenge course, such as high ropes. (For most, walking a balance beam 30 feet above the ground is much different that walking the same beam when it is laying on the ground!) Physically they will be safe, but even so, most will experience some level of fear. And in spite of the fear and perceived danger, most will summon the will to tackle the elements—and feel totally exhilarated about their accomplishments. And the deep seated memory of their courage will provide them long lasting confidence to venture out in all walks of life.

- Make building self-assurance an ongoing area of focus. Hold it up as an organizational value. Talk about it at meetings. Make it part of development discussions and performance reviews. Tell stories about role models, and so forth.

PART 3: ONWARD TOWARD GROWTH

Our real problem, then, is not our strength today; it is rather the vital necessity of action today to ensure our strength tomorrow.
— Dwight Eisenhower

Chapter 13: Thoroughness and Preparation: Maturity

Over the course of this book, we have written about those attributes that are most consistent with people who are able to step up and challenge the conventional ways things are done. Sometimes those challenges are immense and involve a great deal of adversity, even danger.

We did not feel the discussion would be complete without spending some time on the topic of *maturity*. When we speak of maturity, we are not thinking about age or tenure. We are referring to the ability to:

- keep things in perspective
- practice good judgment
- have wisdom
- have a strong sense of values; to know which values are central and inviolable and which might be expendable
- understand the relationship between actions and consequences

Maturity helps a person know when to conform and when not to, when to speak out and when to remain silent. These components of maturity are necessary in all walks of life. They are especially pertinent for those taking risks to affect change or produce growth.

We have all come across people who fly off half-cocked or are incapable of thinking things through very clearly. Inadequate preparation, lack of diligent thinking, erratic or excessive behavior, disregard for consequences, and other questionable behaviors can lead to some very undesirable outcomes, especially when attempting something for the first time. Frankly, it is hard to put much faith in people who frequently act like this.

Every good can have a dark side. Another way to say it is, if taken too far, any strength can become a weakness. Think of a gifted speaker who literally never shuts up or the team that cannot stop preparing and analyzing long enough to ever take action. Or how about Bode Miller in the 2006 Winter Olympics? With great expectations, he failed to place in any race, and even failed to finish a couple. Yet afterwards, he did comment that he still got to party at an Olympic level!

Maturity provides people with the sense to see that extremes do exist and to recognize when they are about to cross into the shadow realm. An occasional venture into the extreme is not uncommon, but being out there too far and for too long will take its toll on anyone, especially on those who are pushing on the outer boundaries of the growth frontier.

Let's consider the extremes of some of the attributes we have already discussed to appreciate why a level of maturity is such a key part of the mix for success.

Passion or Obsession

When does someone move beyond simply having strong passion about something and becoming totally obsessed with it? It is an interesting question, isn't it? How do you delineate the two?

As odd as it may seem, it is a fact of life that two different people can look at the exact same set of circumstances and see entirely different things. It is no different when judging other people, meaning that what you might view as passion, another might see as an outright obsession.

Rather than analyzing the concept of obsession from a clinical sense, our intent is to remind you that there is a difference between having a great deal of energy, enthusiasm, love and desire about something and being totally consumed by it.

Chris Bangle was once asked if he was an artist or a car guy. He safely answered that he was a little of both. Did he have passion about the look of his BMW's? You bet. But he also spoke with a great deal of pride about another of his design team's greatest contributions, outside of their work as car designers. This one was found in the Munich Museum of Modern Design. There, carved out of a 30 ton piece of marble, was a dramatic piece of modern sculpture, created from the curves, bends, ridges and other shapes that went into contemporary car designs. As much as they may love cars, Bangle and his team were not totally driven by just that work. They were able to break away from the demands of the competitive luxury auto world and share their artistic gifts with a larger and different audience than just car buyers.

Some might say that Laird Hamilton takes his passion for surfing too far. After all, he was still out risking his life, even after the birth of a baby daughter. Surfing has always been an integral part of his life. In his own words Laird commented about how he felt most alive when surfing, how it was just part of who he was. Passion or obsession? We feel it best to let his family and friends who know him more intimately answer that question.

Successfully challenging current norms requires thoughtfulness, clear-headedness and awareness of consequences. It is not about being so consumed that you feel it is necessary to take giant risks with reckless abandon.

Vision or Dreamery

Since its release in 2004, many of you have probably seen *The Aviator*, the blockbuster movie, about the life of Howard Hughes. After watching this portrayal of Mr. Hughes, you might have wondered whether he had great vision, or a head full of loose screws.

What does it mean to demonstrate maturity in conceiving a vision? Does it mean being less bold, and opting for a more conservative, predictable future? Does it mean ensuring you have an air-tight plan of execution, before putting forth a desired destination?

It is not hard to build the case that maturity is a necessary part of developing a compelling vision. Randomly putting forth great dreams about tomorrow, without much consideration about reality or consequences is rather foolish. It is difficult to take seriously an individual who deep down believes anyone can actually spin hair into gold, or a major company that believes it can "double in size in the next five years," with no track record or plan to do so. There are many times when it is relatively easy to tell a vision from a fairy tale.

On the other hand go back in time to the early 1970's. Would you have believed enough to invest in some far-fetched notion about operating systems for personal computers, when conventional wisdom said PC's would never be necessary? Might you have considered Bill Gates, Paul Allen and friends from Microsoft more like sci-fi fanatics, who really ought to be getting a college education and pursuing a real job? Sometimes what appears to be complete fantasy turns out to change the world. If we only knew!

Visions are about possibilities—things or events that have never existed before. Unfortunately, there is no solid line that clearly separates a grand vision and complete absurdity. This is why maturity is such an asset. It is also why those who create change spend a lot of time and effort seeking out, studying deeply, debating lively, thinking about, and weighing different possibilities. They put a lot of heart—and mind—into the dreams they choose to pursue.

Confidence or Ego

People who tackle new things need to have a healthy dose of self-assurance.

They need to believe in their own abilities to be successful. But sometimes a person can become too proud to acknowledge the existence of blind spots, and self-assurance becomes only a mask for self deception.

Looking good is a strong driver of behavior in many organizations. We have found that most people want to be viewed as capable opposed to incompetent. They have read and been told that they need to come across as confident in order to inspire others to join in with them. (Is that true for you?) Just be mindful that whether you can convince others of your abilities or greatness is not as important as whether you can convince yourself.

Maturity reminds you about the essential value of self-examination and self reflection. It also reminds you to check in with your internal feelings and not just to rely on external logic. That means that even if others are telling you that you can or you can't, you ultimately have to confront your own feelings and decide if you will or you won't take a step.

There were a lot of logical reasons why Alice Coles should not have possessed the confidence to take on the challenge of moving the community of Bayview across the street. Fortunately, she demonstrated the maturity to freely and publicly confess to all the things that she was neither confident (nor competent) to do, rather than attempting to arrogantly appear as the be all and end all for everything. Alice was confident however, that there were other people who did have the skills and the money necessary to help her community achieve its dream, and that she would be able to find them.

Courage or Fearlessness

Do you consider yourself fearless? Do you think it is healthy to be this way? Would you choose to go into battle with someone who was fearless? Despite catchy T-shirt messages or motivational slogans, "no fear" is not something we have seen as a consistent gene in people who experiment and take the risks necessary to make change happen.

People who step out and try new things experience all kinds of fears. They range from fear of life-threatening, physical danger to the fear of looking bad in front of a group of colleagues. People who successfully challenge find ways to overcome fear, not to deny it.

Maturity helps a person be comfortable enough to acknowledge fear and find ways to deal with it, rather than just injecting loads of testosterone and blindly charging forward. Being fearless means disregarding or dismissing real risks. It can result in acting when you shouldn't. That is not courage. It is foolish arrogance if not plain stupidity.

Think about all of the disciplined training and practice the Apollo astronauts went through to prepare them to land on the moon. The training and preparation enabled them to gain great confidence in themselves, each other, and all the other people and systems supporting them, as they launched into the frightening unknown.

We mentioned earlier how people like to be seen as capable, and sometimes they may try to substitute boldness and daring for competence. We have even come across organizations that seem to encourage raw bravado. And we must admit, it makes a compelling story when a fearless hero goes out with more guts than skill or resources and is successful in slaying the dragon and rescuing the princess. We also believe that admitting to fear and courageously stepping up to confront it, is a more mature and better overall strategy for success.

A Special Obsession

There is one final topic about which we want to remind you that has a dramatic impact on the maturity that people display. For lack of a better term, we will refer to it as being self absorbed—to an unhealthy level.

Think about it. We have all read about people who have had an almost insatiable appetite for a personal agenda, which resulted in very irrational behavior. Sometimes that agenda boils down to basic greed, where an individual is totally fixated on acquiring more and more personal wealth. Other times it might be an infatuation with size, where the goal is making one's company, organization or turf the biggest. Still other times it might be about being seen as a "player" or achieving rock-star or god-like status in what you do.

Here are a couple of examples. In the late 1990's, Wall Street's touting of companies with no rational economic business models or sound plans to become profitable was hardly a mature way to behave. But they were not the only ones caught up in the fray. Think about the investors. Might it have been their desires for immediate riches that caused investors to keep pouring money into firms that they knew were nothing more than shells? So what happened? Market principles changed and speculation became the norm. The key factor was timing—get in, let it ride for a very short time (days or weeks), and then get out. This sounds more like a philosophy for a weekend visit to a gambling casino, which some might say was quite descriptive of the market at that time. There were big winners and there were big losers. And many, perhaps even you, still have much less confidence in the financial markets today because of the recent memory when non-rational forces and a penchant toward easy money or greed ruled the day.

Most of you have probably heard the tale of Dr. Sam Waksal, the founder and CEO of ImClone. (It was ImClone stock that Martha Stewart infamously sold, that ultimately led to her prison term.) Waksal had tax returns showing annual income in the $60 million range. But he also liked expensive art and being seen with or considered friends of famous people like Bill Clinton and Mick Jagger. In fact he had monthly expenses in the neighborhood of $1 million in order to keep up his lavish lifestyle. At the time of this writing, Waksal was in jail, serving time for a variety of illegal acts. Per his own admission, he frequently cut corners and did not pay attention to details. He was solving the bigger problems of creating a drug to battle cancer. Details were for the lesser people. Interestingly enough, Erbatux, ImClone's breakthrough drug, has proven to be a valuable addition in the treatment of cancer, benefiting many. Yet Waksal's excessive behavior which led to a multitude of illegal actions almost drove the company out of business.

You must always remember that turning conventional wisdom on its ear and creating change does not mean taking the law into your own hands and acting in illegal or unethical ways. Questioning the validity of current assumptions, attempting to stretch known physical limits, or thinking about things in entirely new and different ways are much more mature ways of achieving success and achieving new wealth in the long run.

About You

Leading growth and creating new standards requires numerous attributes, which we have brought to light throughout this book. Maturity is one of them. As we have done before, we now invite you to take a moment and examine your own levels of maturity. This is not intended to be a clinical evaluation, but rather to help you assess who you are and connect with some of the motives that prompt you to act in the ways you do.

You will benefit most by looking at maturity from several different vantage points vs. a single overall assessment. For example, we have met powerful, intelligent business people who behave in very mature ways when assessing competing business options, but admittedly become emotionally crippled when attempting to relate with their teenage sons or daughters. Most of us have our moments of greatness and those other moments when we are not so hot.

The reflection questions below are designed to provide you with yet one more way to think about yourself. Be as honest as you can be. And if you are up to it, we encourage you to seek responses from other people. Often times our own blind spots are quite visible in the eyes of others.

1. What do you consider to be some of your greatest strengths? Which of those do you know you use excessively? Which strengths might others say you take to the extreme?

2. What are your emotional triggers—those words, phrases, actions and the like, that for some reason cause you to "go off half-cocked," or react in virtually uncontrollable ways that you usually later regret? How did these triggers develop?

3. In what aspects of your life do you feel inadequate? How do you respond when forced to deal with them? (For example, do you dismiss their importance or raise your voice to sound more convincing? Or do you admit how you feel and seek the advice and assistance of others?)

4. To what extent might you have a personal agenda that you are a bit too pre-occupied with? Is your need to look good or be successful causing you to act in ways (subtle as they may be) that you know are not right for you and others?

5. What are you learning about yourself? What might you need to do to better equip yourself to more willingly approach new opportunities and create change?

6. Do you believe that maturity dampens or stimulates the spirit to challenge norms and test new things? That is, do you believe that as people become more wise and experienced and "know better," they will be more likely—or less likely—to vigorously pursue an idea that is way out there? Which is it for you?

Chapter 14: Moving Forward: What Companies Can Do

Real growth is a tall order for most companies. The Ivory Tower endorses a plan that calls for double digit revenue growth. Their actions reflect the mid-1960's hit by Dusty Springfield—*Wishin' and Hopin'*. Employees gear up for a business building year. Hopes are high. In reality, the company will settle for a 3 to 4 percent increase. Just enough to stifle shareholders and reward top performers with minimal salary increases. Companies are facing a "slow death"—shareholders lack interest, your talent exits for more challenging and rewarding work, and wealth is illusive. The picture is not Dorothy walking down the yellow brick road. Senior management has no one to blame for its circumstances but themselves.

Now, how can organizations take the information offered in this book and begin pursuing real growth—20 to 25 percent annually.

1. It is absolutely mandatory that companies committed to growth have exceptional people in their organization. Now, you are saying to yourself: "what an enlightened statement." Growth companies have exceptional people similar to the people presented in this book. Special situations are inspired by exceptional people. Why are numerous companies settling for ordinary people or are making the decision that deep, intentional growth requires too much time and resources? Growth is difficult work. It takes time, effort and perspiration. Growth requires people to change, improve, and get better. Exceptional people will move, push and drive people to change. This is not an environment that most slow growth managers want to pursue and promote. Slow growth companies are a haven for mediocre performers. They lack key attributes—most notably passion, vision and courage. Such are the decisions that define the future course of companies, careers, and individual and shareholder wealth.

Leaders in companies must walk the hallways, visit the plants, facilitate strategy sessions, interview applicants at all levels, and hang out in the employee cafeteria. These are the activities that will provide the answer to the question, do I have the corporate attributes and character to be a growth company? Don't avoid the evidence. Look hard at each line-of-business, division, department, etc. Does the person who leads this business unit have the attributes discussed in earlier chapters? If your answer has you shaking your head, rolling your eyes, pulling your hair out and kicking yourself, remember this. It has been your choice to avoid hiring the best, to provide minimal training, to offer no coaching and to hold back on the rewards. The accelerator is stuck and there is no growth momentum.

2. Companies generally reflect the character and attributes of their senior leaders. If the company's leaders are passionate and courageous, the organization may be jumping with energy and risk-taking. Conversely, where senior leadership lacks vision, courage and confidence, growth will be lackluster and companies will close their doors easier and earlier. Shareholders will be left with no value for their investment.

Boards of Directors need to make the acquaintance of their senior leadership team and profile their attributes and character. They need to ensure that the senior leadership team possesses the skills and attributes presented in this book. And senior leaders need to be visiting company sites proclaiming the vision and direction with great fervor. They need to gain employee support for risk-taking and change and build confidence throughout the organization. They must also model for others and encourage them to ensure that meetings are full of energy, inspiration and new ideas. Leaders must be credible as generators of hope for people to step up their own efforts around innovation and growth.

3. Most companies have Business Units which meet or exceed "growth targets" every year. This consistent performance doesn't just happen. Study the talent in the high performing Business Units. Is there passion for the products, services, and customer? Are they experienced and knowledgeable about the industry? Are they committed and do they possess the courage to move the business forward in the face of doubts and failure? Are they communicating the vision with great vigor? Do they demonstrate self-confidence in their work? We are sure you will find these attributes residing in growing Business Units. It is your assignment to find out how these "growth" characteristics are able to exist in the Business Unit. Then, replicate it everywhere.

4. Growth is an important goal for every company, division, department and business unit. Shareholders are investing their funds in double-digit growth companies. Companies need to build their core capabilities around growth. Beyond the attributes, the organization needs to identify how employees turn into "growth leaders." Communicate the capabilities at all levels and create development programs. Reinforce them at every opportunity. The capabilities will reflect the attributes and characteristics introduced in this book.

5. Learning is often facilitated through watching other people grow and develop. Actively search for case studies/examples representing the growth attributes and characteristics introduced. Look for unusual situations. Watch for "edgy" representation of risk-taking. Share them with employees at all levels. Affirm with employees that the leaders of the company are promoting innovation and creativity.

6. After you have identified the idea people in the company, you must find opportunities for them to play with their skills and interests. This is a challenge for many organizations. The growth frontier does not attract many employees. It is a risky place filled with many dangers. Insecure people will not last long on the growth frontier. Controlling behaviors are purged and people learn how to work as teams for survival and growth. This is exactly what organizations must allow these people to experience. Try bringing a group together once every month for "turning an idea into an opportunity." Each invited employee will think through a revenue growth idea prior to the meeting. They will market their idea to the rest of the group. If it is selected, a team of four participants will work the idea through a process. On the second afternoon, senior leadership will have the top four ideas presented to them. It should produce incremental revenue and allow the participants to be a part of the "wild, wild west."

7. Growth companies reinforce whatever is needed for ideas to flow continually. Develop and initiate systems and reward programs to support individual efforts in idea generation and operational follow-through. Great ideas have homes. Creating the idea is just the first step. Operational follow-through brings life and organizational value to the idea. Don't allow employee cynicism to block new ideas. Consider this email from a vice president regarding his company's (Fortune 200) morale problems:

> **What is the primary cause for low morale?** *General cynicism to new growth initiatives. Many employees have seen first hand over the past four years the constant errors/operational issues in the company. Unfortunately, it appears that no one is taking ownership of permanently correcting these operational issues and there is no accountability for the person/departments responsible for the errors. Growth has no way of forging forward.*

Encourage whatever behaviors are needed for the organization to grow. People will respond to the opportunities when presented by this challenge.

8. Be patient with this company transition. If you are leading, quarterly results will happen for the organization. Be focused on this transition every day. Anticipate specific behavioral milestones—three months, six months and one year. Understand that instant gratification does not exist in the overhaul of a company's people attributes. Reconstruction of a company's internal growth engine takes a diligent, focused effort.

9. Finally, remember that growth has no value if the appropriate infrastructure and controls are not in place. Frustrations rage internally if growth leaders fail to encourage the spending and development of all the systems, processes and compliance required to support the expansion. The organization must display as much passion for internal operations as revenue growth. The accolades for innovation and community involvement will have meaning only if they are followed-up with the appropriate discipline for internal structural repairs.

The process of spurring breakthrough thinking and new growth opportunities is exciting, energizing, and demanding. Stay with it. The rewards are in front of you. They will be worth the effort.

Chapter 15: Key Lessons: Review and Final Reflections

By the time most people finish reading a book, they likely have already forgotten many of the key lessons to be gleaned from it. We have learned that no matter how many great lessons are printed on the pages of a book, the best lessons come from your own thinking, reflecting and questioning of what you have been reading. Hopefully, you have been doing those things. Perhaps, you have wrestled with many of the questions and concepts, and along the way, written down your responses and ideas, and even your opposing viewpoints.

What have you learned from reading about what a person must have in order to create a different tomorrow through challenge, change, innovation, and growth? We now invite you to take a minute and write down some of the more important things you have learned. This will help you remember the ideas or messages you most want to take with you.

Here are four key points we would like to emphasize, and we hope they will serve you going forward.

1. Business growth and wealth come from change; therefore, you need people who have what it takes to step up and do things that have never been done before. Mergers, acquisitions, even hostile takeovers are certainly ways to expand a business, but they usually are limited in opportunity or profitability. (It is remarkable the number of those business combinations that actually fail to reach their potential.) There is no cap on new ideas however, as Paul Romer explained in his New Growth Theory.

At the time of this writing, there was a lot of hoopla about Google. Since its IPO in mid-2004, its stock price has continued to move upward, reaching the $500 area by year-end 2006. Their operating income was already greater than most of the other established internet companies who had been around a lot longer, like eBay, Amazon and

Yahoo. The question at that time was "is Google worth it?" No one knows if they will have a short run or one day celebrate a centennial birthday. But, even with a lot of favorable press and momentum, they were continuing to keep their foot on the innovation accelerator. Throughout 2006 they continued to offer a steady stream of new, leading edge services. Like all companies, they will have to continue to do so, if they hope to stay around very long.

2. Recognize that not everyone can or will take up the mantle to challenge today's ways of doing things and make the move to initiate change. We believe everyone has the capability, providing they have or develop enough of the characteristics discussed throughout this book. But not everyone will have them to the extent that they will choose to follow through.

For example, if your entire focus is on once again making 10 or 20 or 50 percent more money this period than last, and that goal does not stir the passion of some of your people, don't expect them to be the great creators or leaders of innovative change for you. In the same vein, if you do little to build the confidence of your people, don't look for them to put themselves at risk for you or the organization. You cannot mandate innovation of others, if they are not inspired by or equipped to achieve the desired outcome.

3. Champions of change are not always the role models of everything that is desired in leaders. They have their flaws. They may not be the best listeners or greatest enablers. They can appear dismissive, or unable to relate to the needs of others. You will probably find that they do not follow normal structures, in how they operate or how they communicate. Investing guru, Jim Cramer has been known to rant, rave and throw things. In our interview with Jungle Jim, we found ourselves talking about things that did not appear remotely connected with the questions we asked. And to top it off, we had no idea how we ended up on those topics! Bottom line is that your agenda simply might not be the most important thing to someone seeking to change the world.

We did not say these trailblazers possessed all the noble qualities usually associated with great leaders. The more leader qualities they do demonstrate will undoubtedly be helpful, but they better act with a healthy dose of commitment, competence, self-assurance and maturity if they expect growth and change to occur in their organizations.

4. Never forget that the growth innovations or changes that people pursue, and sometimes stake their reputations on, are very personal things for them. Taking drunk drivers off the road or creating the space tourism industry is not just some organizational goal for Candy Lightner or Burt Rutan. It is an integral part and a measurement of who they are as human beings. If you want people to commit their hearts and souls into breakthroughs that will fuel the ongoing growth of your organization, you must understand the power of these non balance sheet items, such as passion and vision. It is your role to bring them forth in your people and make them an integral part of your company's culture.

Final Reflections

One of the things that we hear most frequently when we talk to people about their aspirations is how in some fashion or another, they want to make the world a better place. We hear it in responses such as, "I want to make a difference in other peoples' lives," or "I want to leave the world a better place for my children and their children." We also hear some responses that might sound a bit more personal and less noble—"I want to do something really cool, I want to leave some kind of memorable mark, or I want to reach my full potential."

We have never heard anyone say, "I want to devote my life to keeping everything exactly as it is. My health and my health care, my relationships with my family and with my colleagues, or for that matter even my cell phone technology is as good as it can ever get. I have no desire to ever have, do, or be anything different." The closest thing we have ever come to this thinking comes from a quote attributed to Charles Duell, the director of the US Patent office in 1899. Rationalizing the suggestion to close the patent office, he apparently remarked, "everything that can be invented has been invented!" Think about that statement for a minute!

It is a fact that people will become overwhelmed and greatly fatigued by too much change. In organizations that are in constant turmoil, people will sometimes wish that things would just stay the same for a little while. This clearly reinforces one of the most basic principles of change, that our perception of the value of change is vastly different when it is *done to us* (as it often is in organizations) compared to when it is *done by us*. No matter how much you might like the dips and loops of the death-defying roller coaster, it can quickly lose its luster, if you can never get off.

Change is a fundamental part of life. Reaching a new level of satisfaction, achievement, wealth or love, requires change. Things are different at that higher level than they ever were before. Change is not the enemy or something to fear—it is the key to our growth and to the fulfillment of whatever goals we set for ourselves, personal or organizational.

For a business to grow, its people must grow. For any kind of growth to occur, change must occur and change comes from people who are willing to push beyond today's norms and standards. We hope that as you set your sights on growing your business, your people and yourself, you will find ways to inspire and increase other peoples' and your own levels of commitment, competence and self-assurance. This is what it takes to create and lead the kind of changes that will make your organization—and perhaps the world at large—a more exciting, profitable, meaningful, and better place.

Enjoy the ride, and thank you for reading our book.

APPENDIX

Acknowledgements

We had many partners in writing this book. We would first like to thank Ken Shelton, our publisher, for his faith in our work. We are extremely grateful for Ken's insights and patience, and for generously offering his knowledge and experience for our benefit. We also want to say thank you to Rick Weiss, who helped create the look and feel of this book. We appreciate his commitment to our work.

There were several people who reviewed our work and served as loving critics throughout the process, offering great feedback and wonderful suggestions. Our special thanks to Georgianne Smith, Janet Collins, Ron Crossland, Jeni Nichols, Liz McKay, Sterling Gross, Paula Cobb, Neal Maillet and Sarah Kaufmann for their help. We are grateful to Warren Church and Miki O'Reilly-Howe from Deskey, Inc., and Dan Johnson and the guys at Eclectic Studios, who provided some valuable insights in helping us think through and better clarify some of our concepts.

We would also like to thank Steve Houchin and Connie Sullivan, our partners at International Leadership Associates, not only for their ongoing support, but for always giving us another way to look at things. And we would like to extend our thanks to Jim Kouzes and Barry Posner, authors of *The Leadership Challenge*, for their friendship, mentorship and encouragement. Their work has inspired a lot of our thinking.

Over the years we have benefited enormously from our partners at the Joy Outdoor Education Center in Clarksville, OH. To Dave Carr, Brandon Allen and all the staff, thank you for providing us and our clients the opportunity to move further into the Growth Zone.

A very special thanks goes to the hundreds of men and women who shared their comments and points of view during our research. We also benefited greatly and learned from many of our client organizations that have embraced and demonstrated the importance of challenging the way things are done to find innovative ways to grow. Luxottica Retail, Fifth Third Bank, P&G, Sandia National Labs, and AT&T are just a few, and we thank them for their support of our work.

And finally a personal message to our spouses—Susan Coats and Patti Heuer. You have been totally supportive over the years as we have pursued our life's vision. This passion for leadership has led us to many different locations to meet with great people in "learning" companies. You have given us the freedom to pursue our dreams. We offer our love and a big, heart-felt thank you for this gift.

Methodology and Sources

For nearly a decade we have asked people to name role models of other people they admired who had been successful at challenging the way things had always been done and achieving some kind of dramatic outcome. These examples were from both business and non-business settings. We then probed deeper to find out what enabled these people to be successful. At first we heard a lot of responses about what these role models did. For example, they did their homework and built solid business cases. They attracted advocates to support them. They created opportunities for small wins and found non-traditional ways to get their agenda's advanced. The one response that was virtually unanimous from all respondents was these role models took risks.

Since taking risks was obviously a cornerstone of challenging things and creating change, we began exploring the question of what someone needed to have in order to do this. What was it that enabled some people to take risks when others would not? What was it that enabled people to take risks on some occasions, but back away on others? We then broadened the scope and began exploring what people needed to have not just to take risks, but to be successful in challenging accepted ways of doing things and creating substantial change and growth. The answers were much different from what people do, and very, very consistent.

We then began searching for and identifying contemporary examples of people who demonstrated great success in breaking away from traditional ways of doing things and re-writing the rules of the game. We studied them and started finding some common traits they all seemed to share that enabled them to be challengers and initiate new changes. We also continued to solicit responses from hundreds of people about their own personal examples of trailblazers and growth champions, this time examining some of the visible traits that people recognized in them.

We then presented many of these cases to more than one thousand people over the years and asked what they believed these role models had to have (not what they had to do), in order to have accomplished what they did. We pooled those responses, which were very consistent with our own findings, and sorted them into the attributes that we have presented in this book. We have continued our research and found that virtually all groups consistently identify the same attributes that they believe people must have in order to challenge current norms and create change and growth.

We need to offer a few additional thoughts about our research. We purposely included examples of all kinds of people involved in some fascinating and inspiring endeavors. Some were well known, while others were not. Some were in a business environment, while others were facing unbelievable challenges outside of the corporate world. But they all accomplished something remarkable.

Our examples came from a variety of sources. We found them in a number of written publications from *Fast Company* to *HBR*, and from more local, lesser know publications and newspapers as well. We studied a seemingly endless number of video interviews from *Sixty Minutes*, *CBS Sunday Morning*, CNBC and other public news organizations. We also conducted personal interviews with people who had led growth breakthroughs in their own organizations. Throughout our research, we constantly reviewed additional secondary information sources, which further detailed the accomplishments and the internal make-up of many of our examples.